UNLOCKING THE CANINE ANCESTRAL DIET

Healthier Dog Food the ABC Way

Steve Brown

Publishing

Wenatchee, Washington U.S.A.

Unlocking the Canine Ancestral Diet
Healthier Dog the ABC Way
Steve Brown

Dogwise Publishing
A Division of Direct Book Service, Inc.
403 South Mission Street, Wenatchee, Washington 98801
1-509-663-9115, 1-800-776-2665
www.dogwisepublishing.com / info@dogwisepublishing.com

Graphic Design: Lindsay Peternell

Disclaimer
This book was written and published for educational purposes only, and it not intended to take the place of veterinary care. Please consult a veterinarian should the need for one be indicated. The author shall have neither liability nor responsibility to any person, pet, or entity with respect to loss, damage, or injury caused, or alleged to be caused, directly or indirectly by the information contained in this book.

Some breeds, such as Dalmatians, can have problems with the purines in beef liver and hearts. Giant breed puppy owners should consult with their veterinarian or their puppy's breeder before making any dietary changes.

Library of Congress Cataloging-in-Publication Data
Brown, Steve, 1948-
   Unlocking the canine ancestral diet : healthier dog the ABC way / Steve Brown.
      p. cm.
Includes bibliographical references.
ISBN 978-1-929242-67-2
1. Dogs--Food. 2. Dogs--Nutrition. I. Title.
SF427.4.B763 2010
636.7'0852--dc22
                                        2009043535

ISBN 978-1-929242-67-2   Printed in the U.S.A.

Make whatever food you feed—dry, canned, frozen or homemade—more like the canine ancestral diet by following the ABCs:

Amount of fat, protein, and carbohydrate based upon the ancestral diet

Balance the fats

Complete the nutrition with fresh foods

FOREWORD

"Let your food be your medicine, and your medicine be your food."
Hippocrates

As a holistic veterinarian, these are words to live by, and *Unlocking the Canine Ancestral Diet,* by Steve Brown, epitomizes this approach to health and well being. In fact, there's so much to like about this book, it's hard to know where to begin.

For starters, Brown's approach is to remind us that dogs are canines, and the wild ancestors of today's domesticated dogs maintained their health by eating certain foods and by eating them in certain ways—thus the "Ancestral" part of the title. Taking this as a basis for formulating a healthy diet with today's food sources, Brown recognizes that today's commercial dog foods are woefully lacking in some dietary needs (especially high-quality proteins); they are especially heavy in others (grain-based carbohydrates); and they are often terribly unbalanced in some nutrients (the ratio of omega-6 to omega-3 fatty acids is typically far too high in commercial foods).

Holistic vets have long talked about the health-gap between what's contained in commercial foods and what dogs should be eating. Most of us advocate a home-fixed diet as a means to compensate for the imbalance of nutrients. But *Unlocking the Canine Ancestral Diet* takes this approach to a new level of scientifically-based sophistication... and even argues that many of our home-fixed menus, while healthier than commercial dogfoods, may actually be out of balance.

Brown has done his homework and is able to present his case for feeding a nutrient mix that more closely matches what has been health food for hundreds of generations of canines. *Unlocking the Canine Ancestral Diet* is chock full of data-filled charts that support his premise that the ancestral diet is good stuff for today's dogs.

Brown then shows how to easily achieve this mix by feeding the correct Amount of fats and carbohydrates based on the ancestral diet; Balancing the fats (creating the correct balance of omega-3, -6, -9's and making sure there is enough DHA in the diet); and Completing the nutrition balance with fresh foods. This ABC program creates a diet that is healthy, balanced, and easy to feed.

Best of all, to make it even easier, Brown shows us how we can achieve a balance of nutrients by feeding his suggested foods only one-day-a-week, whether we are feeding dry, canned, or frozen foods.

And for those of us who want to take the time and effort to go to the next step and feed the ancestral diet exclusively, Brown provides several recipes that use either beef or poultry.

Interestingly, because our home-fixed diets usually contain grain-fed meats (from conventionally fed livestock which produce meats high in omega-6's as opposed to grass fed livestock or wild prey animals that are higher in the needed omega-3's), we are likely feeding an imbalance of omega-6's and -3's, and this book shows us how to correct for that.

The short take on this book is that it is a must read for anyone (and this should include all of us who truly love our dogs) who believes that healthy and nutritious food is the one necessity for maintaining healthy pets. It's a good read, packed with scientifically-backed information, and it presents a practical approach for achieving the goal of helping us to make a healthy diet for our dogs. As easy as ABC.

I will be using this book in my "Fixing Good Foods for Pets" seminars, and I highly recommend it for anyone interested in the long term, overall health of their own best buddies. It would also be a good gift choice for anyone interested in holistic health for dogs, and especially for the veterinarian who still believes that the commercial dog foods he/she sells are all that dogs need.

Randy Kidd, DMV

TABLE OF CONTENTS

INTRODUCTION

"The ABC day made a huge difference," Dr. Doreen Hock told me when I informed her I was struggling to complete this introduction and finish the book. "I could see the improvement in my dogs—and it's easy," she said. "Just tell people to follow the ABCs." What do the ABCs stand for?

- **A** stands for the **amount** of fat, protein, and carbohydrate based upon the *ancestral* diet of the dog. This means *adding* protein to most commercial and homemade foods

- **B** stands for **balancing** the fats. My view is that the health of a dog is dependent on the fats she eats—more than any other nutrient. The importance of the role of fats is something that nutritional experts have just recently established. Unfortunately, some important fats are either left out of commercial dog foods or deteriorate when included in processed, long shelf-life foods.

- **C** stands for **completing** your dog's nutrition needs by feeding some fresh, whole foods.

Follow the ABCs for whatever type of food you feed—dry, canned, frozen, or homemade—and you'll significantly improve your dog's diet, which will increase the odds that your dog lives a healthy, happy life. No doubt about it, and it's as simple as ABC.

The canine ancestral diet

You may have heard of the "Cave Man Diet" as it applies to humans, the theory being that unprocessed fresh foods high in protein and low in carbohydrates are best for people who evolved successfully over thousands and thousands of years consuming just such a diet. The concept of the "Canine Ancestral Diet" for dogs is similar in nature. Dogs and other canids evolved successfully through hunting and scavenging, consuming foods that were not at all like the kibble so many are fed today. Recent nutritional science increasingly supports an ancestral-type diet—high protein, balanced fats, and at least some fresh foods—as the healthiest approach to feeding most dogs.

While in theory one can feed a dog the ancestral diet, in practical terms—given modern lifestyles and busy schedules—it is just not realistic for the vast majority of pet owners. However, there *are* steps you can take to alter or augment what you currently feed your dog to make it more like the ancestral diet and thus improve the nutritional content of your dog's diet.

The ABC way of feeding is based upon detailed analyses of the dog's ancestral diet, supported by up-to-date nutritional science, and my twenty years experience in developing foods for national pet food companies. The ABC plans laid out in the following chapters focus first on correcting the weaknesses associated with modern dog food which generally contain not enough protein, too many carbohydrates, unbalanced fats, and lack the complete nutrition that can only be provided by fresh foods.

There is no need to dramatically change the type of foods you're feeding. If you feed dry foods, for example, you can make *significant nutritional progress* if you make one day a week an ABC day. It's easy, and you'll probably see the difference in your dog within two to four weeks. If you are more ambitious, I have included additional strategies that involve preparing food for your dog that will take you even closer to the ancestral diet. Whatever you choose to do, the ABC way will help improve your dog's diet and overall health.

How this book is organized

This book is intended for a wide audience: dog enthusiasts, veterinarians, and professional dog food formulators. For dog owners wanting a quick and easy way to improve the food they feed their dogs, I have included simple explanations and plans to do so. For veterinarians and professional dog food formulators wanting to know the "why" behind the ABC concepts, I have furnished all the details.

The first three chapters are must-reads for anyone interested in the subject. Chapter 1 details the canine ancestral diet. What dogs ate in the wild prior to the advent of modern dog food represents an ideal diet—primarily consisting of high levels of protein, balanced fats, and fresh foods. This is the gold standard that modern feeders should try to replicate. Chapter 2 compares and contrasts modern dog foods with the ancestral diet with a focus on where modern foods come up short. Chapter 3 provides information on the health benefits of improving the ABCs of your dog's diet, making it more similar to the ancestral diet.

Chapters 4, 5, and 6 are the ABC plans. Chapter 4—designed for dry, canned, and frozen food feeders—presents the ABC day concept. These are relatively simple and easy one-day-a-week plans to make your dog's diet more like the canine ancestral diet. Chapter 5 is designed for readers who are interested in and are willing to devote more substantial amounts of time to preparing meals at home for their dog(s) and who want to understand the underlying science. This chapter provides step-by-step instruction on how to make balanced-fat, ancestral-type diets. Chapter 6 includes three detailed recipes that will help you replicate the canine ancestral diet for your dog(s).

The last two chapters focus on providing more detailed information to readers such as those involved in the dog health and food formulation industries. Chapter 7 discusses in more detail the important topic of proper storage of dry and frozen dog foods. The best dog foods in the world can be ruined, and even become unhealthy, by improper storage. Chapter 8 provides an overview on a variety of subjects including the chemistry of fats for dogs, the dog's need for carbohydrates, high protein diets and their impact on the kidneys, and an introduction to pet food math. I have also included, in the appendices at the back of the book, additional recipes for dogs requiring low fat diets, sources of information, and a recommended reading list. Appendix C includes a list of all abbreviations used in the book.

Tell your friends about the ABCs

As you see the results with your dogs, I hope you will help spread the word about how easy and important it is to feed an ABC day each week. Together, we can help make a lot of dogs healthier and happier, which makes us humans healthier and happier. Thanks.

Readers are welcome to contact me through my website, www.seespotlivelonger.com.

Steve Brown
August 2009

Chapter 1

THE CANINE ANCESTRAL DIET

There is no way of knowing for sure exactly what constituted the diet of the ancestors of the modern, domesticated dog. And, of course, depending on the natural environment (geography and climate) in which they lived, it may have varied considerably. However, there has been a lot of research done on this subject and we do know quite a bit about the diets of the dog's closest wild relatives such as the wolf, coyote, and fox.

One thing that we are quite sure of is that dogs were hunters and scavengers, their diet consisting largely of meat (including some fish) with some lesser amounts of fruit and grasses. Here are summaries from five researchers who have studied the diets of canids in the wild:

> The staple diet of carnivores living in a natural setting includes other animals, carrion, and occasionally fruits and grasses.[1]
>
> Scraps of meat, bones, pieces of carcass, rotten greens and fruit, fish guts, discarded seed and grains, animal guts and head....[2]
>
> Their [wolves] preference is freshly killed meat, but when that's not available, they'll eat anything that could remotely be considered edible.[3]
>
> Wolves typically utilize most parts of an ungulate (hoofed animal) carcass, which is essential for their nutritional demands.

Organs such as the heart, lungs, liver, and kidneys are high in B vitamins, vitamin A, minerals, and fatty acids that are required for maintenance, growth, and reproduction. Some hair is ingested along with meat, which may aid in faster passage through the intestinal tract.[4]

Wolves prefer fishing to hunting, new (2008) research suggests. When salmon is available, wolves will reduce deer hunting activity and instead focus on fish.[5]

Note: details on all footnoted material are listed in the Citations found on page 119.

Based on a review of the literature and my own research, I have concluded that the ancestral diet consisted of about 85 to 90% meat (primarily from whole prey) along with small amounts of fish and eggs, and 10 to 15% scavenged grasses, berries, nuts, and other vegetation. For the estimates of nutrient content, I used the extensive database from Dierenfeld, et al, which includes more than 1,000 analyses of whole mice, rats, deer, chickens, rabbits, reptiles, and amphibians (including organs and glands).[6] The composition of the vegetative portion of the dog's natural diet varied, but probably consisted of easily available foods.[7]

Using these findings, here is what I believe constituted a close approximation to what the canine ancestral diet would have consisted of expressed in terms of foods available today:

85% whole prey*
2 % green leaf lettuce
2 % broccoli stalks
2% apples with skin
2% asparagus
2% cereal grass
1.5% sardines
1% whole egg, including shell
1% spinach
0.5% hazelnuts
0.5% sunflower seeds

*Note that whole prey includes all parts of the prey animal: fur, bones, eyes, tongue, and all the organs and glands.

Nutritional analysis of the ancestral diet

Let's look at this definition of the ancestral diet from a nutritional standpoint. Tables 1.1–1.3 summarize the key findings. Table 1.1 shows that the ancestral dog's diet was a high protein, moderate fat, and low carbohydrate diet.

Table 1.1 Macronutrient content of the canine ancestral diet*

	% of calories	Grams per 1000 kcal**
Protein	49%	123
Fat	44%	49
Carbohydrate	6%	16

*All values have been rounded to the nearest whole number and therefore the total may not equal 100%.

**kcal is short for kilocalorie, which many people refer to as Calorie, with a capital C. A kilocalorie is the amount of energy (heat) needed to increase the temperature of 1 kilogram (kg) of water 1° C. A typical active 45-pound dog consumes about 1,000 kcal per day.

Large amounts of high-quality protein

49% of the calories in the ancestral diet were from protein, primarily from fresh animal sources. Protein from animals, unlike protein from most plants, contains balanced amino acids and a complete range of protein type nutrients, including taurine and carnitine. This protein level exceeds the levels found in all modern commercial dog foods and all of the typical homemade diets I've analyzed.[8]

Dog owners need to be aware that the meat used in most modern dog foods almost always comes from commercial feedlot animals. Not surprisingly, just as wild fish have higher quality fats than farm-raised fish, wild prey animals have higher quality fats than farm-raised animals. They have much higher fat content (therefore less protein per pound) because feedlot animals are sedentary and are fed in such a way to be fattened up. While that is probably obvious in the case of beef and chicken, even smaller domesticated animals such as ducks and rabbits have less protein and more fat in their meat than their wild counterparts.

Moderate amounts of balanced and complete fats

44% of the calories in the canine ancestral diet were from a wide variety of fats. Both the amount of fat and the balance of fats are important. The ancestral diet contained 49 grams (g) of fat for every 1,000 kcal. This amount is close to the mid-range of the National Research Council's (NRC) current recommendation of 21.3-82.5/g for puppies.

Fats represent a broad category of nutrients, just as vitamins and minerals are broad categories. Dogs need to consume the proper amounts of vitamins and minerals, all in a proper balance. Similarly, it is very important that dogs consume a variety of fatty acids—the basic components of fats—in proper amounts and balance. This is a little-known but critical component in the ABC plans.

Before domestication, a dog's diet provided a complete range of fats because the ancestral dog ate many different parts of the prey animal:

- Muscle meat fat contained saturated fats (SFAs), monounsaturated fats (MUFAs), and polyunsaturated fats (PUFAs).

- Storage fat (fat used for storage of excess energy from food) contained primarily SFAs.

- Bone marrow contained primarily MUFAs.

- Organ fat contained primarily MUFAs and PUFAs, with fat protecting organs primarily SFAs, and the fats in brain and eyes primarily PUFAs.

The polyunsaturated fats consumed contained a number of important fatty acids including:

- Linoleic acid (LA), a short-chain omega-6.

- Alpha-linolenic acid (ALA), a short-chain omega-3.

- Eicosapentaenoic acid (EPA) and docosahexaenoic acid (DHA), long-chain omega-3s.

The ratio of omega-6s to omega-3s was between 2:1 and 6:1, within the range now considered optimum by most nutritionists. By contrast, as we'll discuss, dogs today do not normally get access to such a wide range and balance of fats.

It is difficult to estimate the fatty acid balance in the ancestral diet, but based on the evidence I will make the best-educated estimates I can. Overall, combining a lot of disparate data, I believe that the approximate fat balance of the dog's ancestral diet was as follows:

Fats in the ancestral diet, in g/1000 kcal

Total fat:	49 g
Saturated fats:	15–20 g
Monounsaturated fats:	15–25 g
Polyunsaturated fats:	5–15 g

Polyunsaturated fats broken down as follows:

Short-chain omega-6s (primarily LA):	3.5–12 g
Short-chain omega-3s (primarily ALA):	1–4 g
EPA + DHA (long-chain omega-3s):	0.2–1 g
Omega-6/omega-3 ratio:	2:1 to 6:1

Low in carbohydrates

Because of the predominance of meat in their diets, only 6% of the calories consumed by the ancestral dog were provided by carbohydrates, primarily from fruit, grasses, and vegetables. This is substantially below what the typical modern dog consumes—in fact dogs do not even require carbohydrates if they have enough protein available to them. It's not that carbohydrates are so bad per se (see discussion in Chapter 8), it's just dogs can get the nutrition they need without them.

While the ancestral diet itself did not contain high amounts of fiber (defined as a carbohydrate), it did contain fur and other indigestible parts of the dog's prey, which served a similar purpose.

Mineral and vitamin content

The wild prey animals that made up such a significant portion of the ancestral dog's diet contained a higher mineral content than found in modern dog food. The muscle meat, organs, and small glands of wild prey were considerably more mineral-rich than the corresponding parts of today's feedlot-fed animals.

The wild prey animals consumed by the ancestral dog contained greater amounts of antioxidants than in the meat available to most dogs today. Antioxidants are chemical compounds, such as vitamins C and E, that inhibit oxidation. The body produces some of its own antioxidants and some must be obtained from the diet. The polyunsaturated fats in the dog's ancestral diet were consumed with ample amounts of vitamin E and other antioxidants—this makes sense because the dog's prey probably ate nuts, seeds, and other vitamin E rich foods, much more so than present domesticated animals eat. For example, wild duck meat contains 25 IUs of vitamin E per kilogram, while whole domesticated duck has only 10.5 IU/kg.

As shown in the following two tables, the ancestral diet was comparatively rich in vitamins and minerals, exceeding modern nutritional recommendations as set by the National Research Council of the National Academies 2006 Report, *Nutrient Requirements of Dogs and Cats.*

Table 1.2 Vitamin A and E content of the canine ancestral diet, IU/1000 kcal

	Ancestral diet	NRC recommended, puppies
Vitamin A	15,000	1,137
Vitamin E	23	11.3

Table 1.3 Mineral content of the canine ancestral diet compared with NRC standards, per 1000 kcal

	NRC Puppy	NRC Adult	Ancestral
Calcium, g	3	1	5.7
Phosphorus, g	2.5	0.75	3.3
Potassium, g	1.1	1.0	2.0
Sodium, g	0.55	0.2	1.0
Magnesium, g	0.1	0.15	0.4
Iron, mg	22	7.5	43
Copper, mg	2.7	1.5	6.0
Manganese, mg	1.4	1.2	3.1
Zinc, mg	25	15	24
Ca:P	1.2:1	1.3:1	1.7:1

The gold standard

The canine ancestral diet consisted of fresh, high protein, balanced fats, meats, and a smaller amount of fresh fruits and vegetables. As I show in chapters to come, this truly can be thought of as the gold standard of diets for dogs. My task for the rest of the book is to show you a variety of ways to adjust and enhance what you feed your dog so he can enjoy as many of the benefits from the ancestral diet as possible.

Chapter 2

THE THREE WEAKNESSES OF MODERN DOG FOODS

Most modern dog foods come up short in comparison to the canine ancestral diet in three major ways:

1. Not enough protein.

2. Unbalanced and incomplete fats.

3. Can't be completely nutritionally balanced without some fresh foods.

Not enough protein

This weakness is clearly evident in Table 2.1, which compares the percentages of calories derived from the three major nutrients contained in dog foods (proteins, fats, carbohydrates) compared to that of the ancestral diet.

Protein provided 49% of the calories in the dog's ancestral diet, our gold standard. Modern dogs eating typical dry foods get about half as much protein (25% of calories) and seven times the amount of carbohydrate (43% of calories) as their ancestral diet provided. Even dogs being fed typical raw food diets are getting a lot less protein because meat from domesticated, feedlot-fed animals contains less protein and more fat than wild prey animals.

Table 2.1 Percentage of calories from protein, fat, and carbohydrate, various foods

	Protein %	Fat %	Carbohydrate %
Ancestral diet	49	44	6
Typical dry food	25	32	43
High protein dry food	37	43	20
Typical premium-brand canned food	29	50	21
95% meat canned food	31	68	1
Typical frozen commercial raw	36	59	5
Typical homemade raw[9]	36	59	5

Some modern premium dry and canned foods, shown in the table above, attempt to address this shortage by adding more meat. While it does raise the protein level, the downside is that it also raises the amount of fat. Consequently most dogs today consume either more carbohydrate or fat calories than protein calories—and that's a big change over what their ancestors ate.

Unbalanced, incomplete, and, at times, rancid fats

You are what you eat applies to fat more than any other macronutrient.[10]

The scientific evidence is overwhelming—dogs who eat the proper amounts of balanced fats, with a complete range of fatty acids, are healthier and happier. These dogs:

- Learn faster.
- Remember more.
- See and hear better.
- Have fewer skin, coat, and other inflammatory problems.
- Are more coordinated.
- Are less likely to be obese.
- Will probably live longer than dogs who do not consume a proper balance of fats.

Not only is a complete range important, but also the fatty acids must be "defended-from-oxidation." This is important because oxidation causes rancidity.

Most dogs do not eat balanced fat diets, and consume little, if any, docosahexaenoic acid (DHA), probably the most important fat for the brain and eyes. Even most dogs fed homemade diets do not eat the proper balance of fats because modern feedlot animals have different amounts and balance of fats than do wild prey animals. Poorly balanced fats are one of the major weaknesses of almost all commercial and most homemade dog foods. Fortunately, it's easy to correct.

Fats in dog foods

Until recently, nutritionists thought that the primary function of fat was to provide energy, flavor, and deliver vitamins. It was not until the 1980's—more than 30 years after the introduction of commercial dry foods—that canine nutritionists recognized that at least one specific fatty acid, linoleic acid (LA), was essential in a dog's diet.

In 1985, the NRC listed just one fatty acid, linoleic acid (LA), as being essential for dogs. By 2006, however, the NRC had updated its findings and listed five fatty acids as essential: LA, alpha linolenic acid (ALA), arachidonic acid (ARA), eicosapentaenoic acid (EPA), and DHA. I expect that the next NRC update—probably in 20 years—will list gamma linolenic acid (GLA), conjugated linolenic acid (CLA), and probably other fatty acids as essential. These were all fatty acids the dog consumed in the ancestral diet, and these are the fats your dog will consume if you follow the ABC way.

Now, even though the NRC and almost all "fatty acid experts" consider DHA to be an essential fat, the Association of American Feed Control Officials (AAFCO, the pet food regulator), has not yet updated its recommendations and still considers LA to be the only essential fat in dog foods. I think they are hesitant to require DHA in dog foods because, at least with today's technology, these expensive fats are just too fragile to be included in bags of dog food meant to be kept open more than a few days. Fragile fats oxidize, which means they turn rancid. No DHA in the diet is better than rancid DHA.

Essential Fatty Acids (EFAs) for dogs

NRC, 1985	LA, omega-6
NRC, 2006	LA
	ALA, omega-3
	AA*, omega-6
	EPA, omega-3
	DHA, omega-3
AAFCO, 2009	LA

considered essential for puppies

That being said, some dry foods, most often premium puppy foods, do include fish oils, a primary source of omega-3 DHA. The problem is that DHA is very fragile—think fish kept at room temperature. Although the original DHA content of the food is listed on the bag, it is not necessarily the amount of DHA that is in the food when you feed it to your dog. Extrusion processing (where the food is quickly cooked under high pressure, the way most dog foods are processed) and long-term storage make oxidation of the DHA likely. In 2006, the NRC stated, "Many of the PUFAs (polyunsaturated fats, which includes DHA) in the diet such as those from fish undergo peroxidation during processing and storage before ingestion."[11] Peroxidation means the fats turn rancid.

Advances in packaging have reduced, but not eliminated, the amount of oxygen that is transmitted through *unopened* dog food bags. Once the bags are opened, air rushes in and accelerates the oxidation of the fats. All the studies and nutrient analyses tests I've seen on the DHA content of dog foods were conducted at or very close to the time of manufacturing, when the foods were fresh. The tests were not conducted in time frames that reflect *when the dog eats the food,* for instance four months after the dog food was manufactured. Such a time frame might well include three weeks in a hot Houston warehouse, and 20 days after the bag has been opened in the dog owner's sometimes humid kitchen or garage. How much DHA is left under these rough, but typical, conditions? The data I've seen suggest little

DHA is left, and many of the other fats have also turned rancid. This is especially common when large bags of dry food are opened, but not completely consumed, for several days or even weeks.

While we can't always avoid at least some rancid fats in food, we certainly want to minimize the consumption of them.[12] When a fatty acid becomes rancid the shape, structure, function, and activity of the fatty acid is profoundly changed. Rancid fats reduce the nutritive value of the protein, degrade vitamins and antioxidants, and can cause diarrhea, liver and heart problems, macular degeneration, cell damage, cancer, arthritis, and death.[13, 14, 15, 16, 17, 18] It's good policy to avoid feeding rancid fats to our dogs.

My recommendation: the best way for dry and frozen food feeders to ensure the proper balance of fats and to avoid rancid fats is by feeding a properly stored (see Chapter 7), recently made, basic food without added fish oils or EPA and DHA. Instead add these fragile fats yourself, as you will learn in the next chapter on ABC day feeding. The ABC plans provide the essential fats like DHA in fresh, highly usable, non-rancid, natural forms, much better than any bag of dog food.

Can't be complete without some fresh foods

Dogs, like people, need some fresh whole foods. In the past ten years, many long-term studies have shown that vitamins, minerals, and antioxidants from whole foods are more nutritious than the synthesized or refined forms found in most dog foods. Refined nutrients (as opposed to fresh foods) have a role in preventing deficiency diseases, but are not sufficient for best health. They lack the cancer-fighting nutrients found in vegetables and fruit, for example. I discuss this in more detail in my book *See Spot Live Longer*, co-authored with Beth Taylor (www.seespotlivelonger.com).

The canine ancestral diet provided thousands of different micronutrients, some known and many yet to be identified. Scientists are learning that some of the recently-discovered nutrients, including taurine, carnitine, alpha lipoic acid, coenzyme Q10, and many more, are important for overall body and brain health.

For example, the lack of taurine (an important, heat-sensitive, eye, brain, and heart nutrient) in pet foods has a long, sad history. About 30 years ago, before canine and feline nutritionists understood the role of taurine, some cat foods were sold without sources of taurine. Cats, unlike dogs, cannot make any of their own taurine, and must receive all of it in the diet. Thousands of cats went blind and then died before pet food nutritionists understood the cat's need for taurine. But the story does not end there. Pet food nutritionists, based upon tests with Beagles living in laboratory settings, assumed that all dogs did not have a dietary need for taurine.[19] Wrong. It took the early death of hundreds, perhaps thousands, of dogs, including Newfoundlands and Portuguese Water Dogs, who were eating lamb and rice diets before the dog's need for taurine was better understood.

Taurine is now well studied and added to most lamb and rice dog foods, but hundreds of other amino acid and protein type nutrients, all part of the ancestral diet, have not yet been well studied and therefore may not be included in many commercial foods.

In summary

The three weaknesses of most modern dog foods are: not enough protein, unbalanced fats, and a lack of nutrients from fresh foods. Fortunately, it's easy to correct these weaknesses with the ABC day and diet plans. Now that you know what the weaknesses are, turn to the next chapter to learn about some of the many well-documented health benefits of improving the ABCs of the foods you currently feed.

Chapter 3

HEALTH BENEFITS OF
THE ABC PLANS

Amount of fat, protein, and carbohydrate based upon the ancestral diet

Balance the fats

Complete the nutrition with fresh foods

We humans know that if we eat a healthy diet, which includes lean meats, balanced fats, and plenty of fruits and vegetables, we are more likely to live longer, healthier, happier lives. The science is indisputable. The same is true with our dogs. The closer we get to feeding them their ancestral diet, the better off they are.

The health benefits of feeding the ABC plans—whether as an ABC day once a week or full time—are substantial and increasingly well documented. I could fill this entire book just listing the hundreds of reports I studied in developing the ABC plans. Instead, I'll recommend books and websites for those who want to study the issues further at the back of the book and provide citations where I discuss specific studies. For those studies that I think the reader will find most interesting, I have provided a more complete list of references on my website, www.seespotlivelonger.com.

These health benefits include:

- Healthier cells.

- Better brains.

- Better eye health.

- Stronger hearts.

- Keeps extra weight off.

- Less chance of common health problems.

- Lower risk of cancer.

Healthy cells

The balance of fats a dog consumes has a profound influence on the dog's cell membranes—the semi-permeable layers that allow cells to receive nutrients and eliminate wastes. Because every cell in the body has a cell membrane made mostly of omega-6 and omega-3 fatty acids, consuming the proper amounts of omega-6s and -3s has the potential to affect every organ system in the body. A good dietary omega-6/-3 balance, which includes consumption of eicosapentaenoic acid (EPA) and docosahexaenoic acid (DHA), makes the cell membranes fluid, permeable, flexible, and healthy. Too much omega-6 (from chicken fat, corn oil, safflower oil, soy oil, canola oil), on the other hand, makes the cell membranes (including those in the brain) brittle, sluggish, and inefficient. As a result, the dog thinks and moves a little slower. Likewise, too much DHA in the diet can make the cell membranes prone to oxidation, which leads to premature aging.

One recent study demonstrated that the balance of fats consumed affects the expression of the genes, the process in which information from a gene is used to make proteins. The study reported that consumption of a proper balance of omega-6s and -3s reduces the expression of the genes that promote inflammation.[20]

This is why I focus so heavily on making sure that the ABC plans provide dogs the right amounts and balance of fats.

Better brains

Puppies learn faster and remember more, older dogs retain the ability to stay mentally sharp, and all dogs are happier. As I was writing this section, I read a July 2008 report that analyzed more than 160 studies about food's impact on the brain. One researcher, Fernando Gómez-Pinilla, a UCLA professor of neurosurgery and physiological science, concluded that "food is like a pharmaceutical compound that affects the brain," and that DHA, was especially important for improving learning and memory and helping to fight mental disorders. He also stated that getting the omega-3s from food, rather from capsules, is preferable.[21]

Following the ABC plans will improve the functioning of your dog's brain by improving the balance of the fats and providing a complete range of nutrients known to be beneficial for brain health. Improving the balance of fats is most important because the brain is 60% fat, 25% of which is DHA, a long-chain omega-3 fatty acid. Thus, DHA is the nutrient with the most evidence for enhancing intelligence and improving behavior.

A proper balance of fats is especially important for puppies and dogs undergoing training. Studies throughout the world show that for humans—and even rats and mice—an excess of omega-6 shortens attention span and undermines self-control. I believe the same thing happens with all mammals—an excess of omega-6 and insufficient amounts of DHA reduces their ability to learn and remember. DHA is essential for a young mammal's brain development; without sufficient dietary DHA, young mammals do not learn as quickly as those who have sufficient DHA in the diet.

DHA is a major building block of the brain and a critical element in the development of vision and the central nervous system. It is one of the primary fats in the eyes, nerves, sperm, and most rapidly moving parts of animals. The dog's ancestral sources of DHA were parts of prey animals and (if living near fishing villages) fish, fish heads and guts, and aquatic plants (algae, plankton, seaweed). The ABC plans add DHA with sardines and other seafood.

DHA is almost as important for adult dogs in order to keep the brain functioning properly. The adage "old dogs can't learn new tricks" can be true if the dog doesn't consume DHA. Dietary DHA is critical for a dog's brain to have the capacity to grow new tissue and neuron-to-neuron connections, or, in other words, learn new things. Many studies with older dogs show that, with sufficient amounts of DHA and antioxidants to protect them, older dogs are more alert, remember more, and are more capable. In other words, proper DHA consumption helps prevent cognitive dysfunction or "doggie Alzheimer's."[22]

For raw feeders, the ABC recipes ensure that dogs do not consume too much fat—studies with mice suggest that high-fat diets (in which more than 60% of the calories are from fat) can lead to brain deterioration and liver cancer.[23, 24] Fat provides more than 60% of the calories in many raw diets.

In addition to balancing the fats and adding DHA, the ABC plans provide a complete range of nutrients that are reported to help improve brain functions. Phosphatidylcholine, from egg yolks, has been reported to be important for memory, intelligence, and mood. Phosphatidylserine (PS), from sardines, is essential for the normal functioning of the brain's cell membranes, and is involved in memory function. PS supplements have been reported to improve memory function in older people and rats; therefore I expect PS will help dogs as well. Recent research shows that vitamin B12, alpha lipoic acid, and carnitine, which is added by including fresh beef hearts and broccoli stalks in the diet, can help old dogs stay alert as they age.[25]

The ABC plans also promote brain health by adding fresh vegetables and fruits. There is a great depth of science showing that the antioxidants in dark berries help dogs remember what they learn better. Lycopene, from cooked tomatoes, watermelon, and other red foods, help keep the brain sharp. Zeaxanthin and lutein, from raw vegetables, enhance brain function. Luteolin, from celery and green peppers, can reduce brain inflammation. Some flavonoids from raw fruits have been reported to have beneficial effects on the brain even in very small amounts.

Better eye health

Dogs see better and have fewer eye problems as they age. Can following the ABC plans help prevent, or at least delay the onset, of eye problems in older dogs? If fed at a young enough age, yes. I believe that most cases of progressive retinal atrophy and cataracts prevalent in many breeds can be prevented. The data I've seen suggest that if a bitch is fed a balanced fat diet with ample antioxidant protection, the puppies are much less likely to develop eye problems. Great nutrition starts in the womb. For adult dogs, improving the ABCs will probably delay the onset of geriatric eye problems.

In order to maintain good eye health, it is crucial to balance the fats in the diet and provide a source of defended-from-oxidation DHA, the primary fat in the dog's retina. Even if supplemented with DHA, an unbalanced fat diet (for example, high in omega-6s or saturated fats) may promote retinal degeneration, diminishing the dog's ability to see. Lack of DHA in the diet or consumption of oxidized DHA can also be contributing factors to eye problems. The DHA in the ABC plans is from sardines, an excellent source of DHA.

The ABC plans also provide important antioxidants and other nutrients known to protect the eyes. These include lutein from egg yolks (the most usable form of lutein), zeaxanthin, lycopene, vitamins D and E, zinc, and taurine. Multiple studies have found that these nutrients may delay progression of age-related eye problems. The sardines and oysters in the ABC plans provide natural sources of zinc. Taurine, from fresh beef hearts, is also an important eye nutrient for dogs.

Stronger hearts

A stronger heart has many benefits, especially better athletic performance. The ABC plans help build strong hearts by improving the fats and adding nutrients known to benefit the heart. A strong, efficient heart is a key to excellent athletic performances, whether for short bursts like flyball and agility work or for the all day needs of hunting dogs. Balancing the fats and including non-oxidized DHA, as we know from studies with humans, rats, and dogs, are extremely important for proper heart functions. A dietary source of taurine is beneficial for some dogs for proper heart functioning. Some athletes take carnitine supplements to improve their performances; some premium dog foods are now touting "with carnitine" to entice buyers. Other nutrients with known benefits for the heart (provided by the ABC plans) include: alpha lipoic acid, luteolin, vitamin E and ribose, coenzyme Q10 (CQ-10), and polyphenols.

Ribose. Research has shown that ribose is effective in helping the heart function efficiently, and is important for active, working dogs. Ribose is found in fairly high levels in raw red meat, but the cooking process binds the ribose, making it less available. High temperature and pressure extrusion cooking, the way most dry foods are produced, may make most, if not all, the ribose unavailable to the dog.

Coenzyme Q-10. CQ-10 is essential for cellular energy production, and acts as an antioxidant that protects the fatty acids in cell membranes from oxidation. CQ-10 is found naturally in the hearts of ruminants (beef, bison, deer, sheep, elk), which we will be including in the ABC plans. An ABC day for a 25-pound dog (Chapter 4) adds about 11 milligrams (mg) CQ-10.

Polyphenols. These compounds are found in fruits, especially the skins, and in vegetables. They have antioxidant characteristics, which have been shown to help reduce the risk of heart disease.

Keep extra weight off

Dogs stay lean and strong—and lean dogs live longer. Many published studies, led by Purina's long-term research, show that high protein diets (i.e., diets with protein amounts similar to the ancestral diet), help dogs lose weight without losing muscle mass. When we lose weight, we want to lose fat, not muscle mass. The same is true for our dogs. Table 2.1, based upon published Purina research (www.purinavets.com), compares the amount of muscle and fat lost on three different protein level diets.[26] On a low protein diet (20% protein on a dry matter basis—the amount of food left after all the water is removed), one-third of the weight the dogs lost was muscle; on a high protein diet only one-seventh of the weight loss was muscle and 85% of the weight loss was fat. The muscles in the body are made up of protein. The bottom line is that to maintain muscles, the body needs protein.

Table 2.1 Composition and percentage of weight loss at various protein level diets, dry matter basis

Dietary protein %	20% protein	30% protein	39% protein
Muscle weight loss	34%	21%	14%
Fat weight loss	66%	78%	85%

Other studies show that high protein diets and diets containing omega-3 fatty acids help improve the dog's feeling of fullness, so the dog is less of a food pest when dieting, and it's easier to keep her lean. And keeping a dog lean is important—lean dogs live longer. A 14-year life span study by Purina showed that dogs kept lean live longer and have substantially fewer health problems than those who are overweight. The lean dogs lived up to two years longer, developed degenerative bone problems later in life, had stronger immune systems, and had lower blood pressure than heavier dogs.

Following the ABC plans will help dogs stay lean and strong by increasing the protein content of their diets, while providing important nutrients reported to help them stay lean and strong.

Less chance of common health problems

An ABC oriented diet will reduce common canine concerns such as skin allergies, arthritis, and other inflammatory problems. One of the most remarkable studies I read during the research for this book came from Sweden. The study concluded that feeding any homemade or non-commercial foods to a bitch during lactation protected her offspring from subsequently developing skin allergies compared to commerical foods.[27] The odds of the puppies developing skin allergies were twice as high among the offspring from bitches that ate only commercial foods. Hopefully other researchers will replicate the results of this study, and then widely disseminate the message "feed table scraps." But I doubt many dog food companies would want to fund studies showing the health benefits of table scraps!

The best proven dietary approach to reducing inflammatory problems is, once again, to return to our ABCs by feeding the proper *amount* and *balance* of fats, including non-oxidized EPA and DHA, and a *complete* range of antioxidants (often from table scraps) to defend the fats in the dog's body, as discussed in Chapters 5 and 8. Hundreds of peer-reviewed studies published worldwide in human and veterinary nutrition journals (many of which are summarized in the books listed in the recommended reading list), show that the proper balance of fats, primarily the balance of omega-6 and omega-3 fatty acids, can help prevent or reduce in severity all types of inflammatory problems, including arthritis. Consumption of EPA has been shown to be effective in reducing inflammation; hence it is often called the anti-inflammatory fat. EPA is found in all cell membranes and is needed to make critical inflammation-moderating messenger chemicals called eicosanoids. If the dog's cell membranes contain adequate levels of EPA, the body will respond to minor infection or injury with an appropriately mild, fast-resolving inflammatory reaction, rather than the excessive, persistent inflammation produced by the eicosanoids made from low omega-3 content diets. One of the best sources of EPA is snake oil. Snake oils, despite their reputation in the United States as bogus, are often effective in reducing joint pain. Fortunately, sardines and other fish are also good sources of EPA.

Other studies, focusing on just DHA, show that long-term consumption of it helps reduce the pain and inflammation on joints. Balancing fats and adding DHA does not act like a drug that immediately reduces pain. Please don't expect to feed an ABC day and see your creaky old dog be agile again in a few days. As the fats in the cell membranes are turned over (a process that can take weeks to years depending upon the type of cell), the DHA replaces some of the omega-6s in the cell membranes, making the membranes more flexible and improving joint movement. While most dogs will show some improvement in a few months, be aware that older dogs may not. DHA consumption will slow down the progression of degenerative diseases, but not necessarily reverse it.

Compared with the amount of fat in a dog's ancestral diet, most dogs are fed dry foods that lack fat (Table 2.1). That's why several formal studies and much anecdotal evidence suggest that adding *any* fat or oil to a dog's diet often helps the skin and coat of many dry dog food fed dogs. Raw diets are high-fat diets—perhaps that's one of the reasons why most raw-fed dogs appear to have healthy coats. The ABC plans make the amount of fat in a dog's diet more like the ancestral diet, which will result not only in a healthy coat, but in overall improved health.

Lower cancer risks
Welcome words for any dog owner—your dog is less likely to get cancer if fed the proper diet. In my first book, *See Spot Live Longer,* I discussed some of the many studies showing that the consumption of vegetables and fruits exerts protective effects against cancer, the number one disease killer of dogs. Since then, more detailed and long-term studies continue to show that consumption of vegetables (especially vegetables like broccoli) protect humans, mice, and dogs from cancer.[28] All the ABC plans include fresh vegetables.

Consumption of green vegetables is especially important for dogs who eat dry foods. Dry foods are susceptible to aflatoxin (a highly toxic substance produced by some molds) contamination. Even though small amounts of aflatoxin are considered acceptable in the grains used for dog foods, with lesser amounts allowed in human foods, green vegetables can help offset its negative effects. Green vegetables contain chlorophyll and have been shown to help delay the onset of symptoms of liver cancer caused from consumption of aflatoxin-contaminated grains.

Of course, improving the fat balance and consuming non-oxidized DHA helps protect against cancer since the fats consumed affect every cell in the dog's body. Following the ABC plans and my advice on storing foods in Chapter 7 will also help ensure that a dog consumes fewer rancid fats, the consumption of which, as we've seen, may contribute to cancer.

Chapter 4

AN ABC DAY FOR DRY, CANNED, AND FROZEN FOOD FEEDERS

One day a week is all I ask. Make one day a week an ABC day and with about ten minutes of preparation, you'll significantly improve the overall nutrition of your dog's food. It's easy to do and these three steps will address the major weaknesses in most commercial dog foods:

> **A**dd high-quality protein with hearts, eggs, and sardines

> **B**alance the fats with sardines

> **C**omplete the nutrition with hearts, eggs, sardines, and vegetables

The ABC day plans

I have developed two ABC day plans depending on what you currently feed your dog. **ABC1** is for those who feed traditional dry foods that typically provide less than 30% of calories from protein. The ABC1 plan for traditional dry foods adds protein and fat, thereby reducing carbohydrates. **ABC2** is for those who feed the higher fat, higher protein dry foods (e.g., Evo™, Barking at the Moon™), most super-premium puppy foods, high meat content canned foods, and frozen raw diets. Foods in the ABC2 group already have sufficient amounts of fat, the plan therefore adds protein and helps balance the fats without increasing the fat caloric contribution (the percentage of calories coming from fat).

Tables 4.1 and 4.2 below list the ingredients and amounts to feed based on your dog's weight for the ABC1 and ABC2 day plans respectively.

Table 4.1 ABC1 plan, for most dry dog foods

Dog's weight	5-pound	15-pound	25-pound	50-pound	100-pound
Beef hearts, oz	3	4	6	10	16
Sardines, 3.75 oz cans	1/2	1	1 1/4	2	3
Eggs (large, no shells)	1/2	1	2	3	5
Vegetables and fruits, oz	1	2	4	6	10
Calories (kcal)	230	395	600	940	1,500

Table 4.2 ABC2 plan, for higher fat and protein foods

Dog's weight	5-pound	15-pound	25-pound	50-pound	100-pound
Beef hearts, oz	3	5	7	11	16
Sardines, 3.75 oz cans	1/2	1	1 1/4	2	3 1/2
Egg whites	1	1	3	4	7
Egg yolks	1/4	1/2	1	2	3
Vegetables and fruits, oz	1	3	4	6	10
Calories (kcal)	230	405	600	930	1,500

One day a week, replace what you normally feed with the appropriate ABC day plan, making it a grain-free, commercial food-free day. If you want to feed treats on the ABC day, use nuts, pieces of meat, or small pieces of vegetables and fruits, but no grains.

These plans make enough food to feed typical adult dogs for one day, providing 14% of the weekly caloric needs of typical adult dogs. Active dogs will need more food—increase the amounts of the ABC plan accordingly. Double or triple the listed amounts for young puppies and lactating moms, but do not feed more than once per week. These recipes are not for full time feeding—so if you get excited about this and want to switch to a full time feeding ABC plan, please see Chapters 5 and 6.

If your dog is not accustomed to a variety of foods, introduce fresh foods slowly over a couple of days. For example, add 1 oz of hearts on the first day, an egg on the second day, and sardines on the third. The next week try the full ABC day as shown in the charts above. When feeding an ABC day, there is no need to add other vitamin, mineral, or fatty acid supplements to your dog's food, even on the non-ABC days, unless advised to by your veterinarian.

ABC day ingredients and preparation

Beef hearts
Sliced beef hearts are readily available (especially if you ask), are relatively inexpensive, high in protein, low in fat, and are a great source of:

- Taurine.
- Carnitine.
- Coenzyme Q-10.
- Ribose.
- Conjugated linoleic acid (CLA).
- Gamma linolenic acid (GLA).
- Trace minerals.
- And other nutrients.

If you can find them, choose grass-fed or pasture-raised beef hearts. If you can't find beef or other ruminant (lamb, buffalo, deer) hearts, you can substitute chicken or turkey hearts, or beef kidneys. You can also substitute liver for up to 50% of the heart, but not more than 50% to prevent an excess of vitamin A. I usually specify organic filtering organs (liver, kidney, spleen) because organs from organically raised animals should have fewer toxins than those from commercially raised animals. Kidneys are a good source of carnitine and contain an amino acid-type nutrient, gamma-aminobutyric acid (GABA), which is reported to be a brain and eye nutrient.

Beef hearts are a great source of taurine and carnitine. Cut the beef heart into small pieces and serve raw or lightly cooked. While I serve the hearts raw to my dogs, lightly cooked—leaving the center raw, is certainly okay. Light cooking kills any pathogens that may be present. (If they are present, pathogens are usually on the outside surface area of the heart, not within the heart.) I emphasize lightly cooked only because high heat processing reduces taurine and carnitine bioavailability, destroys the enzymes, and reduces the overall nutrient value of the hearts.[29]

Just as taurine was an overlooked nutrient in dog foods for many years—and dogs suffered as a result—canine nutritionists are now learning that lack of carnitine (another amino acid-type nutrient) may be a contributing factor to heart disease and obesity in dogs. Has lack of carnitine in dry foods shortened some dogs' lives? Probably, just as the lack of taurine in some lamb and rice diets shortened the lives of many dogs. The ancestral diet contained ample carnitine from fresh, raw meats, but processing removes significant amounts of it.[30] Some dog food manufacturers are now touting "added carnitine" to entice people to buy their foods, but this is at best a band-aid approach, even if the added carnitine is stable in opened bags of food. Taurine and carnitine are two of probably hundreds of amino acid-type nutrients found in fresh raw meats, most of which have not yet been studied. I'm sure next year we'll learn about other nutrients that dogs need to be at their best, but extrusion processing and long storage times destroy. Dogs need some fresh meat, no doubt about it.

Sardines

Sardines in water with no salt added are the best for dogs. Those in olive oil are also acceptable, but, for the healthiest fat balance, avoid sardines packed in soy or other omega-6 rich oils (see Table 8.2). If the plan calls for 1¼ cans of sardines, it is okay to feed two cans in one week of the month, and the other weeks feed just one can. Use up the can of sardines within two days after opening it so that the DHA does not go rancid.

Sardines and other fish are the best way to add the long-chain omega-3s, including DHA. Many of the studies showing the significant body and brain benefits of EPA and DHA have been conducted with fish oils; good fish oils are effective, but I prefer sardines for many reasons.

Sardines are a sustainable fish with low mercury loads. When added to your dog's diet, they provide highly-absorbable, defended-from-oxidation DHA, EPA, arachidonic acid (AA) and other fatty acids. Sardines are a great source of protein, and they provide a complete range of trace minerals including iodine and natural forms of zinc, a full complement of vitamins including D, B12, and E (including gamma tocopherol and the tocotrienols), antioxidants and other known and, I'm sure, unknown nutrients. The triglyceride and phospholipids forms of DHA found in sardines are more absorbable and stable than the ethyl ester forms in most fish oils, and may be more effective than fish oils for improving brain functions and preventing cancer.[31, 32] (Some of the more expensive brands of fish oils have revised their processes so that most of the DHA is in a triglyceride form; look for these if purchasing fish oils.) In the ancestral diet, the DHA and EPA were primarily in triglyceride and phospholipid forms; I think it's wise to keep it that way. In short, whole foods are almost always more nutritious than refined products.

You can substitute canned wild Alaska pink salmon (the bones are edible), oysters (a great source of zinc, especially important for pregnant and lactating females), and other fresh, frozen, or canned wild fish for sardines. Pacific oysters are probably better than gulf oysters, which may have too much mercury, and certainly safer than canned oysters from China. Some pet food manufacturers provide fresh frozen ground sardines; these are great when fresh, but the grinding accelerates the oxidation of the fats, so the shelf life is limited. *Never feed raw salmon or trout,* especially Pacific salmon, because it may contain a microbe that can kill dogs. Pacific salmon often carry a worm, called a trematode, which itself carries a microbe, Neorickettsia hilmonthoeca. The trematode lives in the intestine of many fish-eating birds and mammals (including cats), with little ill effect. Dogs, however, can get very sick and die from the microbe within the trematode. Deep freezing kills the trematode; however I am not sure that deep freezing kills the microbe and therefore I recommend not feeding raw salmon to dogs.[33]

If you or your dog do not like sardines or other seafood, feed the hearts, eggs, and vegetables once a week, and add a recently-produced (look for expiration dates) fish oil plus three ground almonds for every gram of fish oil. The vitamin E in the almonds is necessary to help protect the DHA in the dog's cells from oxidizing (see Chapter 5 for more information). Without the sardines, the caloric content of the ABC boost is reduced by 185 kcal per can of sardines. To make up for the loss of calories, add about ½ cup of dry food. One gram of fish oil and 3 almonds adds 30 kcal.

Eggs

I recommend using commercial eggs for ABC feeding. However, eggs from true free-range chickens are usually more nutritious than commercially raised eggs, with better fat balances and more vitamin E.[34] It's not necessary to use the more expensive omega-3 or DHA enriched eggs, because we're adding the DHA with the sardines and therefore enriched eggs are probably not worth the extra cost.

The plans differ mainly in the use of egg whites and yolks. In ABC1, I use the yolk and whites, while in ABC2, to reduce fat, I use the whites and only a fraction of the yolk. To compensate for the calories provided by the yolks, I increase the amount of hearts and vegetables in ABC2. For ABC1, you can serve the eggs raw or lightly cooked, but for ABC2, with more egg whites than yolks, I recommend lightly cooking the whites by placing the eggs in the shells in hot water (just short of boiling) for 30 seconds, light poaching, or cooking the egg sunny side up. Keep the yolks raw and whole, not scrambled.

Note that there is no consensus of opinion on the best preparation of eggs. Some researchers are concerned with a substance called avidin contained in egg whites. It is thought to interfere with the body's absorption of some of the biotin in the yolk. Cooking egg whites prevents this problem, but changes the structure of the proteins in the cooked egg whites. Other researchers believe that it is not necessary to cook the whites because the yolks have more than enough biotin to overcome the biotin losses, and therefore the eggs should be served raw. While dogs have no reported problems with cholesterol, if you scramble and cook the yolk, the cholesterol may oxidize. Oxidized cholesterol, like oxidized fats, is not healthy for dogs. Cooking the yolks also significantly reduces the lutein content. Lutein is an important nutrient for the eyes.

Try to scrape the inside of the shell so you can use the membranes. These membranes contain glucosamine, chondroitin sulfate, and hyaluronic acid. These nutrients are reported to help relieve joint and soft tissue pain.

Fresh eggs provide important brain, eye, and body nutrients in natural, unprocessed forms. They should be part of every dog's diet, especially pregnant bitches. There are four parts to eggs, and we're going to use three of these parts: whites, yolks, and the membranes on the inside of the shell—but not the shells. Egg whites are the perfect protein and provide riboflavin, magnesium, potassium, selenium, and zinc. Egg yolks contain essential fats, including: conjugated linoleic acid, phospholipids, choline, lutein, vitamins D, and (along with the sardines) a full range of natural vitamin E compounds, including cancer-fighting gamma tocopherol and the tocotrienols. Egg membranes contain nutrients that can help relieve joint pain. While eggshells provide a source of calcium when properly prepared (washed and finely ground), we do not need to use the shells with the ABC day plans.

The eggs, along with the sardines and fresh greens, provide a natural source of vitamin K. The 2006 NRC's *Nutrients Requirements of Dogs and Cats* considers vitamin K to be an essential nutrient. However, the AAFCO does not, so not all dog foods contain vitamin K. There is some debate about the safety of supplemental forms of vitamin K, so it's best for your dog to consume natural forms.

Vegetables and fruits

Feeding a variety of colorful vegetables and fruits will provide the best defense against cancer, the number one disease killer of dogs. Finely chop, juice, or lightly cook the vegetables and mix with the hearts, sardines, and eggs.

Most of the micronutrients in dry dog foods come from human-synthesized vitamins and minerals. Take a look at the last 20 ingredients on almost any dog food and they normally consist of synthesized nutrients. Synthesized vitamins and minerals have been shown to prevent short-term deficiency diseases, but they do not provide optimum nutrition, and lack many of the cancer-fighting compounds found in vegetables and fruits. Vegetables and fruits provide hundreds of different types of antioxidants and other beneficial plant compounds that are not in most long shelf-life foods.

Here are some suggestions for which fruits and vegetables to choose.

- Dark berries provide nutrients that are important for proper brain development.

- Red watermelon is an excellent source of lycopene, a potent antioxidant that protects the heart and other organs.

- Beets contain powerful antioxidants that help prevent the breakdown of vitamin E.

- Orange foods, such as carrots, cantaloupes, and sweet potatoes, fed raw, provide antioxidants that protect the eyes.

- Spinach, kale, and collard greens are rich in trace minerals and contain antioxidants that help the brain, eyes, and body.

- Green leafy vegetables contain boron, another brain nutrient.

- Cruciferous vegetables (especially broccoli) have the most proven anti-cancer fighting properties. Many of these nutrients are fat-soluble; you should therefore feed them as part of a meal that contains fat.

Green vegetables are especially important for dogs who eat dry foods. Dry foods are susceptible to aflatoxin contamination and small amounts of aflatoxin are considered acceptable in most dog foods. (See my book, *See Spot Live Longer,* for complete details.) Green vegetables contain chlorophyll, which may help delay the onset of symptoms of liver cancer caused from aflatoxin-contaminated grains.

For the most micronutrients for your dollar, feed human leftovers such as broccoli stalks and watermelon rinds. The stalk has about the same vitamin and mineral content—and better fats—than the broccoli flower, and is often thrown away. Watermelon rinds contain citrulline, a newly discovered nutrient that is reported to help the heart, circulation, and immune system.

Your dog won't be able to take full advantage of the nutrients in the vegetables and fruits unless you juice, finely chop using a food processor, or (with some vegetables) lightly cook them. A rigid cell wall, composed primarily of cellulose, surrounds plant cells. Cellulose is very difficult for dogs to digest. It is the contents of the cell itself, not the cellulose wall that provides most of the nutrition. Unless the cell wall is broken, most of the nutrients are not available.

Raw or lightly cooked? Some nutrients are more available if you feed the vegetable or fruit raw, and some more available if you lightly cook the food. Lightly cooking (steaming for a short amount of time) may help improve the dog's ability to absorb some of these nutrients. Some research suggests that broccoli should be lightly cooked; the cooking reduces the amount of compounds that block the absorption of nutrients. Cooking tomatoes increases the amount of lycopene that humans can absorb. This is probably true with dogs as well. Other data show that cooking decreases the quantities of flavonoids (including lutein and zeaxanthin) vitamin C, and destroys almost all the polyphenols. If you are cooking the vegetables, the shorter the cooking time, and the lower the temperature, the less the reduction in most of these nutrients.

My recommendation on the cooking versus raw issue here is to cover both bases. Lightly cook some of the vegetables some of the time, and feed them raw some of the time.

What foods *not* to feed

Avoid onions, which in large amounts can cause a form of anemia. Grapes and raisins, even including those grown with no insecticides, fertilizers, or antifungals, have been reported to cause kidney failure in some dogs, but the reasons why are unknown. Macadamia nuts may be toxic for some dogs, even in small amounts. Chocolate may be a problem for some dogs.

Some dogs are allergic to yeast products. If you give your dog any type of yeast (some people believe that brewers' yeast and garlic helps repel fleas), watch your dog carefully. Dogs with a history of systemic problems like ear and skin irritations may have an allergy to yeast and should probably stay away from it. As discussed earlier, raw Pacific salmon and west coast trout can have microbes that are deadly for dogs, and should be avoided.

The results: more like the ancestral diet

Just one ABC day per week provides your dog with additional high-quality protein, improves the balance of the fats, and adds hundreds, perhaps thousands, of nutrients that were part of the canine ancestral diet and that are not usually available in commercial dry foods. In other words, you will move much closer to the "gold standard" of high protein, moderate-to-high-fat, low-carbohydrate content diet.

The following three tables below show how the one ABC day improves the protein, fat, and carbohydrate content of the diet for 25-pound dog. For those feeding typical dry foods (Table 4.3), an ABC day increases the protein by 15% and decreases the carbohydrate caloric contribution by 12%, which is significant. Tables 4.4 and 4.5 show the changes when an ABC day plan replaces high protein dry foods and typical raw foods. In all cases, an ABC day makes the diet more like the ancestral diet.

Table 4.3 ABC1 with traditional dry foods, protein, fat, and carbohydrate caloric contributions

	Ancestral diet	Typical dry	6 days dry, 1 day ABC1	Changes
Protein	49%	26%	30%	+15%
Fat	44%	32%	34%	+6%
Carbohydrate	6%	42%	37%	-12%

Table 4.4 ABC2 with high protein dry food, protein, fat, and carbohydrate caloric contributions

	Ancestral diet	High pro dry	6 days dry, 1 day ABC2	Changes
Protein	49%	37%	40%	+10%
Fat	44%	42%	41%	-3%
Carbohydrate	6%	21%	19%	-10%

Table 4.5 ABC2 with typical commercial frozen raw chicken diet, protein, fat, and carbohydrate caloric contributions

	Ancestral diet	Frozen raw	6 days frozen, 1 day ABC2	Changes
Protein	49%	36%	39%	+10%
Fat	44%	59%	57%	-3%
Carbohydrate	6%	4%	4%	NM

An ABC day for a 25-pound dog provides 125 grams of high-quality protein by adding three excellent protein sources: egg whites (the perfect protein), beef hearts, and sardines. These foods improve the amino acid balance of the overall diet by providing 1 gram (abbreviated g) of methionine and 3 g of lysine, two of the limiting amino acids with dry foods, and a complete range of protein-type nutrients often not be available in dry foods, including carnitine and an estimated 250 milligrams (abbreviated mg, a milligram is 1/1000 of a gram) of taurine.

An ABC day provides 1.2 g of well-defended-from-oxidation DHA in phospholipid and triglyceride forms, the most stable and usable forms, to improve the fat content and balance in your dog's diet. Recent research suggests that DHA in these forms may be 9 times more absorbable than the ethyl ester forms found in many fish oils.[35] If these studies are correct, 1.2 g of DHA in sardines may be the equivalent of 5–10 g of DHA from fish oil. Since salmon, and most other fish oils, are about 20% DHA, the absorbed amount of DHA in one and one-quarter, 3.75 oz of sardines may be equivalent to the absorbed amount in 25–50 grams of fish oil.

The ABC day also adds 0.7 g of eicosapentaenoic acid (EPA), 0.1 g of docosapentaenoic acid (DPA), two long-chain omega-3 fatty acids; and 0.4 g of alpha-linolenic acid (ALA), a short-chain omega-3, for a total of 2.4 g of omega-3 fatty acids, all in natural forms.

The ABC day provides 2.7 g of omega-6 fatty acids, including 0.8 g of arachidonic acid (AA), a long chain omega-6 fatty acid, and the primary fat in the brain. AA is important for brain and nerve development, but since it is expensive and fragile (oxidizes readily), it is often not included in adult dog foods. We've added 1.9 g of linoleic acid (LA), a short chain omega-6 fatty acid. Other fats we've added include conjugated linoleic acid (CLA) and gamma linolenic acid (GLA) from grass-fed beef hearts.

The ABC day improves the important omega-6 to omega-3 ratio of the overall diet. While the fatty acid composition of commercial dry dog foods varies substantially, on average, most high quality dry dog foods have omega-6 to -3 ratios in the 7:1 range.[36] As shown in Table 4.6, ABC day improves the ratio to 4.7:1, putting it in more in line with recommended ratios (2:1 to 6:1) and the ancestral diet.

Table 4.6 Omega-6/-3 ratios

Dry food	6 Days Dry, 1 Day ABC	Ideal
7:1	4.7:1	2:1 to 6:1

Moving closer to the canine ancestral diet

As we've seen, an ABC day each week adds protein, helps balance the fats, and provides a complete range of nutrients not available in long shelf-life foods. And I recognize that for most busy pet owners, doing one day a week will be as much as many people can handle. If you are in this group, give yourself a pat on the back because you are doing a lot for your pet.

For those of you who want to put more time and energy into your dog's nutrition, there are more benefits for your dog as you try to replicate a "perfect" diet. In order to do this however, you will need to make your own food and feed it to your dog full time. That's what the next chapter is about.

Chapter 5

THE THREE KEYS TO MAKING ABC RECIPES

"The best way...is to feed a raw diet that mimics the evolutionary norms of canines."[37]

—*Dr. Ian Billinghurst*

If you want to feed the very best and are willing to spend the time necessary to make your own dog foods for full time feeding, this chapter is for you. Now you are going to learn the details about how to build ruminant (beef, lamb, venison, buffalo) and poultry based recipes that meet the **ABCs: ancestral amounts of protein, fat, and carbohydrates; balanced fats; and complete nutrition.** These details will be of interest principally to those readers who want to understand the logic and science behind the recipes. If you want to proceed directly to the recipes without the detailed background information you can skip directly to Chapter 6.

The three keys to building ABC diets are:

1. Start with lean meats.

2. Balance the fats.

3. Balance the minerals and vitamins.

Start with lean meats

If you want to mimic the ancestral diet and balance the fats in your dog's diet, it's important that lean meats provide the base of the recipes. Today's domesticated feed animals, such as cows and chickens, have more fat and less protein than do wild prey animals, so it's important to remove some of the fat or feed only lean parts. Table 5.1 lists the amount of protein and fat per 1,000 kcal of many types of meat used for homemade dog foods. As you can see, some cuts of meat—such as 80% lean ground beef and chicken necks with the skin and fat—have about half the protein and twice the fat of the ancestral diet. The most important step in building ancestral type diets is to select lean meats.

Table 5.1 Protein and fat of various meats compared with ancestral diet, g/1000 kcal

	Protein	Fat
Ancestral Diet	**123**	**49**
93% Lean Beef	145	49
90% Lean Beef	119	59
80% Lean Beef	69	80
Chicken thighs w/skin (no bone)	85	75
Chicken thighs w/o skin (no bone)	175	35
Thighs: ½ w/o, ½ w skin	117	61
Chicken necks w/bone, w/o skin*	130	42
Chicken necks w/bone, skin & fat	51	96
Necks: ½ w/o, ½ w/skin	77	78
Turkey necks	108	63

*may provide excess of Ca, see pages 51-52.

Lean meats also have higher mineral concentration than fatty meats, because the minerals are in the protein, not the fat. Table 5.2 shows that 93% lean ground beef has more than twice the amount of many trace minerals than 80% lean ground beef. The listed trace minerals are those that are often not sufficient in homemade dog foods that use fatty meats.

Table 5.2 Trace mineral content, 93% and 80% lean ground beef, mg/1000 kcal

	93% lean	**80% lean**
Iron (Fe)	16.2	7.8
Manganese (Mn)	0.07	0.04
Copper (Cu)	0.5	0.2
Zinc (Zn)	34.6	16.8

So as a general rule, when feeding beef, use 90–93% lean. When feeding chicken parts, such as necks, backs and thighs, remove the skin and separable fat from half to three-quarters of the parts.

I also recommend serving the meat raw. However if you are not comfortable with that, you can lightly cook the meats—without the bones—before mixing in the other ingredients. Bones, ground or whole, should only be served raw.

Balancing fats

Once you choose the lean meats, the next step is to balance the fats. This is not an esoteric detail—in fact I've come to believe that providing complete and balanced fats is just as important as providing complete and balanced minerals and vitamins. The fats the dog eats affects the health of every cell in the dog's body.

In this section, I'm going to show you how to balance:

1. The saturated and polyunsaturated fats.

2. The short-chain omega-6s and -3s (LA and ALA).

3. The long-chain omega-3s (EPA and DHA).

It's much easier than it looks, but only if you're feeding lean meats.

Here's the ideal fat balance, based upon the fat balance of the ancestral diet:

The ideal fat balances (g/1000 kcal)

Amount	49 g
Saturated fats (SFAs):	15-20 g
Monounsaturated fats (MUFAs):	15-25 g
Polyunsaturated fats (PUFAs):	5-15 g
LA (short-chain omega-6):	3.5-12 g
ALA (short-chain omega-3):	1-4 g
LA/ALA ratio	2:1 to 7:1
EPA + DHA (omega-3s):	0.2-1g
Overall omega-6/omega-3 ratio	2:1 to 6:1

Step 1: Rotate ruminant and poultry meats to balance the saturated and polyunsaturated fats.

Most domesticated ruminant meats contain too much saturated fats (SFAs) and insufficient amounts of polyunsaturated fat (PUFAs), as shown in Table 5.3. On the other hand, this table shows that even the leanest chicken parts (chicken necks with all the skin and fat removed) have 13 g of polyunsaturated fats per 1,000 kcal, close to our recommended maximum of 15, leaving little room to balance the fats by adding the essential omega-3 PUFAs, including DHA. The last row in Table 5.3 shows that rotating the chicken and beef provides a much better balance of fats than feeding either alone. (MUFAs are monounsaturated fats.)

Table 5.3 Fat balance, g/1000 kcal

	SFAs	MUFAs	PUFAs
90% lean beef	21*	21	2**
Chicken necks w/o skin	13	16	13
½ 90% lean beef & ½ chicken necks w/o skin	20	22	6

recommended amount 15–20
**recommended amount 5–15*

Step 2: Add oils appropriate for the meat sources to balance the short-chain omega-6s and -3s.
Since domesticated feed animals often do not contain a healthy balance of fats, it's usually necessary to balance the short-chain omega-6s and -3s, primarily the omega-6 linoleic acid (LA) and the omega-3 alpha linolenic acid (ALA), by adding specific fats from sources such as hempseed and flaxseed. Poultry (chicken, turkey, duck, pheasant) and ruminant (beef, buffalo, lamb, venison) meats have different fat balances and require different approaches.

The balance of omega-6s and -3s the dog consumes has the potential to affect the health of every cell and organ in the body. Adding the wrong fats for the meat source (i.e., flaxseed oil to beef, or sunflower, safflower, soybean, and corn oils to chicken), can make a fat imbalance worse, and health problems can result—sometimes quickly. These fat imbalances may be diagnosed as allergies or food intolerances to flaxseed or to beef, but it's just an easily correctable fat imbalance. Table 5.4 shows the LA/ALA balance of beef with various oils, Table 5.5 shows the LA/ALA balance of chicken with various oils, Table 5.6 shows the omega-6/-3 ratio of various chicken parts, and Table 5.7 summarizes the best oils or foods to add and not to add for poultry and ruminant recipes.

Balancing fats in beef

As I noted above, beef is high in saturated fats (SFAs) and low in polyunsaturated fats (PUFAs). This means that beef, even fatty beef, does not meet minimum requirements for linoleic acid (LA), an essential omega-6 fatty acid, and alpha linolenic acid (ALA), an essential omega-3. Obviously, oils need to be added to improve the fats.

Here's where it is easy to make a mistake by adding the wrong oils to beef foods, especially by those dog food makers wanting to add omega-3s. Corn oil increases the LA content, but puts the important LA/ALA ratio deep in the unhealthy range. We can do much better and we can do worse. Let's look at what happens when flaxseed oil is added. Flaxseed oil adds sufficient ALA, but not enough LA, and results in an omega-6 to -3 ratio below recommendations. This may be unhealthy. Hempseed oils, on the other hand, provides LA and ALA, and produces almost a perfect omega-6/-3 ratio. Hempseed oil also contains GLA, a conditionally essential fatty acid, which means that most dogs can make enough GLA to meet their needs most of the time. But, when working hard or under stress, some dogs cannot make enough GLA and need a dietary source.

Table 5.4 Short-chain omega-6/-3 93% beef with various oils, g/1000 kcal

	LA, Omega-6	ALA, Omega-3	Ratio
93% lean beef	1.5*	0.2*	6.5:1
+ 1 tsp hempseed oil	4.6	1.2	4:1
+ 1 tsp corn oil	4.5	0.3*	16:1*
+ 1 tsp flaxseed oil	2.2*	2.9	0.8:1*

does not meet standards

With beef foods, including pasture-raised animals, always examine linoleic acid first, before adding omega-3s. Without sufficient LA, increasing the omega-3 content with flaxseed, chia, salmon, and other omega-3 containing oils can do more harm than good. Linoleic acid was the first fatty acid to be considered essential, because lack of LA presents health problems rather quickly, often showing first in the skin and coat.

Rule of thumb to balance the fats in ruminant recipes: add 1 teaspoon (4 g) of hempseed or walnut oil, two tsp of ground hemp-seeds, or 2–3 tsp of canola oil; and ¼ of a 3.75 oz can of sardines, in water or olive oil, per 1–1¼ pounds of 90–93% lean meats.

Balancing fats in chicken

Chicken parts, as we've seen, are high in polyunsaturated fats, especially linoleic acid (LA), a short-chain omega-6 fatty acid, therefore, in chicken recipes, we do not want to add any other foods or oils rich in linoleic acid, such as soybean, safflower, sunflower, canola, walnut, wheat germ, or hempseed oils. Some of these oils are good for beef foods, but they are not good for chicken foods. Do not add any foods, seeds, or oils containing LA to chicken foods, instead add alpha-linolenic acid (ALA) rich ground flaxseeds or flaxseed oil.

Some people advise against the use of flaxseed, believing that many dogs are allergic to flaxseed. However, in many cases I suspect that it is not the flaxseed or oil itself that causes the symptoms of allergies; it may be the fat imbalance, created by adding the omega-3s from flaxseed to beef products without adding an omega-6 source that causes the problems.

Table 5.5 Short-chain omega-6/-3 ratio, lean chicken w/oils, g/1000 kcal

	LA, Omega-6	ALA, Omega-3	Ratio
Chicken breast w/skin	11	0.4*	26:1*
+ 1 tsp corn oil	13	0.4*	29:1*
+ 1 tsp flaxseed oil	11	2.7	11:1*
+ 1 tsp hempseed oil	13	1.2	11:1*

does not meet standards

Rule of thumb to balance the fats in poultry recipes: remove most of the skin and fat; add 1 teaspoon (4 g) of flaxseed or chia seed oils, or 3 tsp of freshly ground flax or chia seeds; and ¼ of a 3.75 oz can of sardines, in water or olive oil, per 1–1¼ pounds of lean chicken.

Table 5.6 Following the chicken rule of thumb, using thighs, g/1000 kcal

	Ancestral diet	Recipe
Total fat	49	46
Saturated fats	15-20	11
Monounsaturated fats	15-25	15
Polyunsaturated fats	5-15	13
LA, omega-6	3.5-12	7.5
ALA, omega-3	1-4	3.2
LA/ALA	2:1 to 7:1	2.4:1
EPA + DHA	0.2-1	0.9
Overall omega6/omega-3 ratio	2:1 to 6:1	2:1

Table 5.7 Fats to add and not to add to lean meats

	Lean Poultry	Lean Ruminant
Oils or whole foods to add		
	flaxseed	hempseed
	chia seed	walnut
	sardines	canola
		sardines
Do not add		
	corn	flaxseed
	safflower	chia seed
	soybean	
	sunflower	
	hempseed	
	fish oils	

Step 3: Add sardines or other fish to provide a complete range of fats, including EPA and DHA.

The third step to balancing the fats is to provide an antioxidant-rich source of DHA. Many people add fish oils, but, as I discussed in Chapter 4, I believe that sardines, cooked wild salmon (*not* raw), and other wild, fatty fish are better for dogs than fish oils. This is especially true when making your own foods because sardines are an excellent source of trace minerals, including iodine, which are often left out of many homemade diets.

Adding fat, even a few grams of fish oil, without adding minerals is probably not a good idea. Compared with the ancestral diet, modern diets—dry, frozen, and homemade—are often mineral short. Minerals are needed to help metabolize fats; adding fat to a food without adding minerals can impair fat absorption, throw off the fat/mineral balance, and can lead to mineral deficiencies. Sardines, on a caloric basis, are one of the most mineral-rich foods available.

Sardines provide antioxidant protection for the fats that you will not find in most refined fish oils. When we eat fresh nuts, seeds, or fish we consume the oils and hundreds of different types of antioxidants with the oils. The antioxidants protect the oils in the food and after we eat them, if the food is fresh, they also protect the fats in our cells from oxidation. Refined oils, though, do not offer the same level of defense against oxidation. During the refining of oils the protective package is removed and many of the antioxidants are destroyed. A few antioxidants, usually vitamins A and E, are added back in primarily to protect the fatty acids in the container; these antioxidants are slowly (or rapidly for poorly packaged products) used up protecting the fragile fats in the container, and therefore there may not be sufficient antioxidant protection for the dog's internal needs.

EPA and DHA, like most nutrients, provide wonderful health benefits in small amounts, and are detrimental in excess amounts. Feed small amounts (0.2–1 gram of EPA +DHA per day for a 45-pound dog) and you'll probably make your dog smarter and healthier. Feed much larger amounts and your dog will probably slow down mentally and age at a faster rate.

Special caution: the gallon-sized, clear container of fish oils.
At dog shows I've seen gallon-sized, clear, milk-jug type plastic containers of fish oil. Perhaps if one has a lot of large dogs, the price per serving may be appealing, but these containers scare me. The lightweight plastic provides little barrier to air and transmits light, which causes photo-oxidation. Unless you know the manufacturer and the freshness of the fish oil, and have enough dogs to use up the gallon very quickly, I advise you to avoid fish oils in plastic, see-through containers.

Balancing minerals and vitamins
The third key to building excellent recipes is to balance the minerals and vitamins. Here are my recommendations:

1. Ensure proper amounts of calcium and phosphorus for boneless and bone-in recipes.

2. Provide other essential minerals, focusing on iodine, manganese, copper, iron, and zinc, by adding vegetables and other mineral-rich foods.

3. Consider vitamins D and E, but don't worry about water-soluble vitamins.

Ensure proper amounts of calcium and phosphorus
Calcium (Ca) and phosphorus (P) are often called the "macrominerals" in that they are the two minerals that the dog needs in the largest quantities. We measure the Ca and P content in grams per 1000 kcal. When formulating dog foods, it's important to ensure that there are proper amounts of calcium and phosphorus, in the proper ratio.

If you feed your dog a homemade recipe based on ground beef he will not be getting enough calcium or the proper ratio of calcium to phosphorous as shown in Table 5.8.

Table 5.8 Ca and P, amounts in ground beef, g/1000 kcal

	Ca	P	Ca:P
80% lean ground beef	0.1*	0.6*	1:6*
90% lean ground beef	0.1*	1.1	1:11*
95% lean ground beef	0.1*	1.6	1:16*
Standards			
NRC puppy	3.0	2.5	1.2:1
NRC adult	1.0	0.8	1.3:1
Ancestral	5.7	3.3	1.7:1

does not meet any standards

Solution: Add 1.5–2% bonemeal

The easiest way to insure your dog gets enough calcium and is getting the proper ratio of calcium to phosphorous is to add bonemeal to ground beef based recipes. The amount added should equal 1.5–2% of the weight of the meat. Table 5.9 shows the results of adding bonemeal as recommended.

Table 5.9 1.5% bonemeal (typically 29% Ca and 13% P) compared with standards, g/1000 kcal

1.5% bonemeal added to	Ca	P	Ca:P
90% ground beef	2.6	2.2	1.4:1
93% ground beef	3.0	2.6	1.3:1
Standards			
NRC puppy	3.0	2.5	1.2:1
NRC adult	1.0	0.8	1.3:1
Ancestral	5.7	3.3	1.7:1

Rule of thumb: If you're feeding 93% or leaner meats, add 1.5% bonemeal, or one heaping teaspoon per pound of meat. This meets puppy and adult recommendations. If you're feeding 85–90% lean meats, add 1.5% for adults and 2% for puppies.

Many calcium rules of thumb are not accurate

Many meat without bone recipes call for the addition of 1–2% of the weight of the meat in eggshell powder, plant-based calcium, or other calcium-only sources to meat in order to provide the proper amounts of calcium and phosphorus and the proper Ca:P ratio. This rule of thumb does not work if you're trying to: (1) meet NRC puppy recommendations; (2) mimic the ancestral diet; or (3) if you're feeding fatty meats. I'm not saying that the meals produced using 1–2% eggshell powder are bad—very healthy dogs fed for generations with these recipes speak for themselves. If we're striving for perfection, though, we can do better.

To meet NRC puppy recommendations and ancestral amounts, one needs to add Ca and P to meats without bone, and base the amount added on the fat content of the meat. Bone is, after all, primarily Ca and P, and bone provides about one-half of the phosphorus in prey animals.[38]

In Table 5.10, I add eggshell powder at the rate of 1% of the weight of the meat (that would be 4.5 grams per pound of meat). This is because eggshell powder is a good source of Ca, which the meat lacks. Note that this 1% rule will satisfy requirements for adult dogs if you use lean meats. However, if you're feeding puppies or aiming at the ancestral diet this calcium source does not meet recommendations. For puppies, you must use a calcium source that also provides phosphorus—like bonemeal—as discussed above.

Table 5.10 1% eggshell powder added to lean meats is acceptable for adult dogs, g/1000 kcal

1% eggshell powder added to	Ca	P	Ca:P
80% lean ground beef	1.5	0.6*	2.4:1*
90% lean ground beef	2.2	1.1	2:1
95% lean ground beef	2.8	1.5	1.9:1
Standards			
NRC puppy	3.0	2.5	1.2:1
NRC adult	1.0	0.8	1.3:1
Ancestral	5.7	3.3	1.7:1

does not meet any standards

Simply adding 2% eggshell powder to lean or fatty meats obviously increases the Ca, but then the ratio of Ca:P is not balanced, and there is still not enough P for puppies, as shown in Table 5.11.

Table 5.11 2% eggshell powder added to any meats creates a Ca: P imbalance, g/1000 kcal

2% eggshell powder added to	Ca	P	Ca:P
80% lean ground beef	2.9	0.6*	4.8:1*
90% lean ground beef	4.2	1.0	4.2:1*
95% lean ground beef	5.4	1.5	3.6:1*
Standards			
NRC puppy	3.0	2.5	1.2:1
NRC adult	1.0	0.8	1.3:1
Ancestral	5.7	3.3	1.7:1

does not meet any standards

Bone-in poultry recipes: watch out for too much Ca and P

For bone-in chicken and turkey recipes, a diet of primarily lean necks and backs contains too much Ca and P, as shown in Table 5.12. To match the Ca and P content of the ancestral diet, the lean bone-in parts should be only 40—60% of the meat content of the diet, with the rest of the meat being lean boneless meats.

Table 5.12 Calcium and phosphorus content, g/1000 kcal

	Calcium	Phosphorus
Ancestral diet	5.7	3.3
AAFCO maximum	7.1	4.6
100% lean chicken necks	12.4	7.0
50% lean necks, 50% lean boneless	5.3	3.2

Review other essential minerals

Essential minerals are the chemical elements required for life, and must be provided by the diet. The essential minerals for dogs are divided into the macrominerals, measured in grams per 1,000 kcal, and trace minerals, measured in milligrams (one thousanth of a gram), and micrograms (one millionth of a gram) per 1000 kcal. The NRC considers the following minerals essential for dogs:

Macrominerals:

- Calcium
- Phosphorus
- Magnesium
- Sodium
- Potassium
- Chloride

Trace minerals:

- Iron
- Copper
- Zinc
- Manganese
- Selenium
- Iodine

The trace minerals boron, chromium, molybdenum, silicon, nickel, and vanadium are considered essential for humans, but not yet considered essential for dogs.

One key to providing complete and balanced minerals, once again, is to feed lean meats. They are much more mineral-rich than fatty cuts as was shown in Table 5.2. The other key is to insure organs comprise 15-20% of the meat content. Without the organs, it is not possible to get sufficient minerals in the diet without resorting to human-synthesized forms. When making lean meat diets that include some organ meats, recipes for puppies are often only short in manganese, iron, zinc, and iodine, and sometimes copper and sodium. As discussed below, recipes for adult dogs are less demanding.

Properly prepared vegetables can help provide most of these minerals. See Chapter 4 for a discussion on how to choose and prepare vegetables for dogs and for a list of foods that should NOT be fed to dogs. Vegetables provide minerals, vitamins, antioxidants, and other beneficial plant compounds, including fiber. The dog's ancestral diet included fur and indigestible parts of its prey. While not defined as fiber, these parts served a similar function. Since we're not feeding fur, it's important to include fiber. In the recipes in Chapter 6, the vegetables provide the fiber, and in the perfect fat recipe (Recipe #3 on pages 81-82), the optional use of oat bran provides additional fiber.

Manganese is an essential trace mineral that must be considered in every recipe. It's usually the first trace mineral that I consider because it's the most difficult to reach standards, and most of the whole food manganese sources I add also contain iron, copper zinc, and often iodine. In the recipes below I add manganese with a combination of spinach, yams, broccoli, flaxseed, hempseed, kelp, and oat bran. The USDA website, http://www.ars.usda.gov/Services/docs.htm?docid=17477, lists other manganese-rich foods.

After working out the manganese sources, I look at the copper, iron, and zinc. Quite often, the manganese sources add sufficient amounts of these minerals to meet NRC recommendations. When feeding beef liver, one rarely needs to consider other copper sources.

It's wise to always ensure a source of iodine, which is essential in very small amounts: a 45-pound dog needs 0.22 mg per day. The best sources include iodized salt, kelp, oysters, sardines, and other seafood. The data on iodine content of foods are sparse and unreliable. The amount of iodine in meat and vegetables is dependent upon the soils in which they were grown, what the animals ate, and other factors. I recommend, therefore, including one or two of the iodine-rich foods mentioned above, and to rotate the sources. For example, in the beef recipe in Chapter 6, I include one can of sardines and 2 teaspoons of iodized salt per 5 pounds of food.

Consider vitamins D and E

It's important to feed some vitamin D rich foods, especially in the winter, for indoor dogs and dogs with long, dark coats that block the sun. Dogs can make some of their vitamin D needs from sunlight, but only if they get to lay out in the sun and their coat isn't so thick that it blocks all the sun's rays. In all the recipes, I include several vitamin D rich foods, including sardines, oysters, eggs, and liver. Diets without at least two of these ingredients may be short in vitamin D.

The amount of vitamin E necessary in a diet is dependent upon the amount and type of polyunsaturated fats fed. The more polyunsaturated fats the dog consumes, especially the highly unsaturated fats like EPA and DHA, the more vitamin E protection the dog requires. The National Research Council's 2006 report recommends adding between 0.9 (for ALA) to 1.8 mg (for DHA) of vitamin E for every gram of that fatty acid fed to protect the dog's cell membranes from suffering oxidative damage, as shown in Table 5.13.

Poultry foods, high in PUFAs, require more vitamin E than do beef foods. In the recipes below, I calculate the amount of vitamin E necessary based upon the PUFA content and recommend adding a natural-sourced vitamin E supplement. Natural sources are always listed in the "d" form: d-alpha-tocopherol. Don't use synthetic dl-alpha-tocopherol. Many companies offer natural-sourced vitamin E complexes that, like almonds, include a full range of tocopherols and tocotrienols.

Table 5.13 Estimated minimal requirement of vitamin E (alpha-tocopherol) needed to compensate for elevated vitamin demand caused by some common unsaturated fatty acids[39]

Fatty acid	Double bonds	Vitamin E/g fatty acid
Oleic	1	0.09
Linoleic (LA)	2	0.60
Alpha-linolenic (ALA)	3	0.9
Arachidonic (AA)	4	1.2
Eicosapentaenoic (EPA)	5	1.5
Docosahexaenoic (DHA)	6	1.8

In the ABC recipes in Chapter 6, I add EPA and DHA by feeding sardines, which have ample antioxidant protection. If, instead of sardines, you add fish oil to your dog's food, vitamin E requirements increase. My recommendations, based upon the NRC's numbers, are to *add three freshly crushed raw almonds for every gram of fish oil.* Recent studies show that almonds, containing vitamin E and other antioxidant compounds, help reduce damage from oxidation, while some studies suggest that vitamin E alone is less effective.

If you follow recipes similar to my recipes, with lean meats and some vegetables, you do not need to concern yourself with the water-soluble vitamins. The recipes provide ample B vitamins and vitamin C.

Chapter 6

BUILDING BEEF AND CHICKEN ABC RECIPES, STEP-BY-STEP

In this chapter I'm going to show you how to make excellent home-made dog foods *for full time feeding* that closely mimic the ancestral diet. There will be three recipes: one based on boneless ruminant meats; a second based on bone-in poultry meats; and a third which contain both poultry and ruminant meats, what I call the perfect fat and protein recipe. These recipes are for all life stages, which means they meet the NRC standards for puppies and pregnant and lactating moms as well (which are more demanding than the standards for adult dogs). In some instances I will provide ingredient alternatives for adult dogs.

Please note that the nutrient content of all natural foods upon which these recipes are based can vary significantly. Therefore the nutritional content data presented below may vary somewhat from what you may actually experience. I am confident, however, that if you follow the steps closely you will be feeding your dog a very healthy diet.

The key steps you need to follow are similar between the two recipes. However, there is one important difference. For the boneless ruminant recipes, the six steps are:

1. Choose lean meats.

2. Balance and complete the fats.

3. Ensure proper amounts of calcium and phosphorus.

4. Add vegetables and other mineral and antioxidant rich foods.

5. Review the fats.

6. Review vitamins D and E.

For the bone-in poultry recipes, the six steps are:

1. Choose lean meats.

2. Ensure proper amounts of Ca and P.

3. Balance and complete the fats.

4. Add vegetables and other mineral and antioxidant rich foods.

5. Review the fats.

6. Review vitamins D and E.

The difference between the two is when you balance the fats. When working with bone-in poultry recipes, the calcium and phosphorus source–the meat with bone–also contains fat. I find it best, therefore, to ensure the proper amounts of Ca and P first, before balancing the fats. The opposite is true with the ruminant recipes.

Recipe #1: Ruminant beef

4 pounds, 90–93% lean ground beef
¾ pound ground beef heart, preferably grass-fed
¼ pound beef liver, preferably organic or grass-fed
1 pound spinach, lightly cooked or finely ground raw
½ pound broccoli stalks or other vegetable, lightly cooked or finely ground raw
1 can (3.75 oz) of sardines, in water (no salt added)
1½ ounces human-grade bonemeal
4 teaspoons (16 g) hempseed oil
2 teaspoons (8 g) iodized salt

This 4,000 kcal recipe will feed a typical 25-pound adult dog for one week and a typical 45-pound dog for four days. It is about 16 oz of food a day for a 25 pound dog; 27 oz a day for a 40 pound dog.

Step 1: Choose lean meat

- *Four pounds of 90–93% lean ground beef.*

- *¾ pound ground beef hearts and ¼ pound beef liver (preferably organic).*

In the analyses below I use two pounds of 90% lean and two pounds 93% lean ground beef. If you're feeding pregnant or lactating bitches, or puppies, it's best to use only 93% lean. You can substitute lean ground lamb, bison, or venison if you want.

One pound of organs is 20% of the meat content and 15% of this recipe. Hearts, as discussed in the ABC day, provide an excellent source of protein, minerals, and other nutrients. Liver is a good source of trace minerals—including copper, iron, manganese, iodine, and zinc—and a reliable source of vitamin D. Liver should be no more than 7.5% of a dog's overall diet, otherwise the diet may contain too much vitamin A. Filtering organs, such as livers, kidneys, and spleens, remove toxins from the blood and into the urine or intestines to be excreted. I think it's best, but certainly not essential, to feed naturally raised or organic sources for all filtering organs.

Step 2: Balance fats, add complete range of fatty acids

- *Four teaspoons hempseed oil or 1 ½ oz of freshly ground hempseeds. Or as an alternative, four teaspoons of walnut oil or eight teaspoons of canola oil.*

- *One can of sardines (3.75 oz), in water, no salt added.*

As discussed above, the best oils to add to beef, bison, and other ruminant-based foods are hempseed, walnut, and canola. These oils provide LA, short-chain omega-6s, and ALA, short-chain omega-3s. For this recipe, we're adding four teaspoons (16 grams) of hempseed oil or 1 ¼ ounces of freshly ground hempseeds. If you can't find hempseeds or oil, add 4 teaspoons of walnut oil or 8 teaspoons of canola oil.

The can of sardines adds highly usable forms of EPA and DHA, making the fatty acid balance acceptable (as shown in Table 6.1), and we can move on to finish the recipe. We'll check the fat balance again after we add the vegetables and other mineral-rich foods.

Table 6.1 Good fat balance: 4 lbs beef meat and organs with 4 tsp hempseed oil and one (3.75 oz) can of sardines, g/1000 kcal

	Ancestral diet	Recipe
Total fat	49	50
Saturated fats	15-20	19
Monounsaturated fats	15-25	19
Polyunsaturated fats	5-15	6
LA, omega-6	3.5-12	4.2
ALA, omega-3	1-4	1
LA/ALA	2:1 to 7.1	4.2:1
EPA + DHA	0.2-1	0.3
Overall omega-6/omega-3 ratio	2:1 to 6:1	3.6:1

Step 3: Ensure proper amounts of calcium and phosphorus

Bonemeal—equal to 1.5% of the weight of the lean meats from step 1.

The next step—when developing formulas for meats that do not include bone—is to add Ca and P. I usually use human-grade bonemeal, but you can also use dicalcium phosphate. As discussed above, many homemade diets do not properly balance the Ca and P, because the mathematics involved can sometimes be difficult, and there is a lot of inaccurate information on the Internet. With boneless ruminants, I examine Ca and P after I balance the fats, because nutrients are best evaluated on a caloric basis, and the meats and fats provide most of the calories.

A safe rule of thumb is to add 1% (of the weight of the meat) bonemeal to lean meats to provide the proper amounts of Ca and P for adult dogs, and 1.5% for puppies. For this recipe, I'm adding 1½ oz of bonemeal to the 4 pounds of meat to meet NRC standards for puppies. Most natural food stores sell lead-free bonemeal or MCHA.

Table 6.2 shows the mineral content of our recipe with meats, fats, and bonemeal. I've asterisked the two minerals, manganese and iodine, that we need to consider next to meet standards.

Table 6.2 Mineral content compared with standards, beef recipe after meat, fats and bonemeal, per 1000 kcal

Mineral	Unit	NRC adult	NRC puppy	Ancestral	Recipe
Calcium (Ca)	g	1.0	3.0	5.7	3.6
Phosphorus (P)	g	0.75	2.5	3.3	2.8
Potassium (K)	g	1.0	1.1	2.0	2.1
Sodium (Na)	g	0.2	0.55	1.0	0.5
Magnesium (Mg)	g	0.15	0.10	0.4	0.18
Iron (Fe)	mg	7.5	22	43	18
Copper (Cu)	mg	1.5	2.7	6.0	3.9
Manganese (Mn)	mg	1.2	1.4	3.1	0.2*
Zinc (Zn)	mg	15	25	24	28
Iodine (I)	mg	0.22	0.22		0.02*
Selenium (Se)	mg	0.09	0.09	0.5	0.12

does not meet standards

Step 4. Add vegetables and other mineral-rich foods

- *One pound of spinach.*
- *One half pound of broccoli stalks.*
- *Two teaspoons of iodized salt.*

Since we're feeding lean beef and beef liver, which is rich in copper, most of the trace minerals the dog needs are at recommended levels for adult dogs, with the exception of manganese and iodine. For puppies, we also need to consider sodium and iron.

I always solve the manganese shortage first. In this recipe, we'll use spinach, which also adds the additional iron and vitamin E necessary for puppies. In the next recipe we'll use kelp and in the third recipe we'll use oat bran.

We're adding 1 pound of spinach and ½ pound of broccoli stalks, served lightly cooked, juiced, or finely chopped with a food processor. The vegetables also provide a source of fiber.

Some dogs do not tolerate spinach well and may develop kidney stones or have difficulty urinating if fed spinach. Check with your vet if you think this might apply to your dog. If you determine that you should not feed spinach, you will need to find another source of manganese, iron, and vitamin E. You can substitute one pound of green leaf or romaine lettuce—but that will only solve part of your manganese shortage. You can make up the difference by adding:

- 3 mg of manganese in the form of a supplement, or

- 2 oz (before adding the water) of oat bran, or

- ½–2 teaspoons of high manganese content kelp meal (brands vary), and eliminate the iodized salt added below.

If you are feeding puppies and do not use spinach, you will want to add 10 mg of iron, preferably by substituting ¼ pound of the heart recommended with ¼ pound of spleen (if you can find it) or an iron supplement. To meet NRC vitamin E recommendations, add 3 freshly ground almonds or 20 International Units (usually 1 drop) of a natural vitamin E supplement.

For iodine, I add two teaspoons (8 g) of iodized salt, with 0.1 mg iodine per gram (Morton Salt datum). Instead, we could add kelp, but we're using kelp in the next recipe and kelp (which can have a high arsenic content) should probably not be fed everyday. The sardines, oysters, and beef liver are reliable sources of iodine, but may not have sufficient amounts to meet NRC recommendations for these recipes. Therefore, to be safe, I'm adding iodized salt—one teaspoon is probably sufficient—adding 2 teaspoons guarantees the recipe will meet NRC recommendations.

Table 6.3 shows the complete mineral content of this recipe and compares results versus both NRC recommendations and the ancestral diet. Note that the recipe now meets NRC mineral recommendations for all life stages.

Table 6.3 Mineral content: beef recipe with spinach, broccoli, and 2 tsp iodized salt, per 1000 kcal

Mineral	Unit	NRC adult	NRC puppy	Ancestral	Recipe
Ca	g	1.0	3.0	6.2	3.6
P	g	0.75	2.5	3.6	2.8
K	g	1.0	1.1	2.0	2.9
Na	g	0.2	0.55	1.0	1.4
Mg	g	0.15	0.10	0.4	0.29
Fe	mg	7.5	22	43	22
Cu	mg	1.5	2.7	6.0	3.9
Mn	mg	1.2	1.4	3.1	1.4
Zn	mg	15	25	24	28
I	mg	0.22	0.22		0.23
Se	mg	0.09	0.09	0.5	0.12

Step 5. Review fats

Before we finalize the recipe, let's review the fats again, because the addition of vegetables and other foods can change the fat balance. Table 6.4 shows that the fatty acid balance is right where we want it to be. Because this recipe is in the low part of the desired polyunsaturated fatty acid (PUFA) range of 5–15 g/1000 kcal, this recipe is ideal to rotate with high-PUFA content chicken foods, which we will discuss next in Recipe #2.

Table 6.4 Fatty acid balance after adding vegetables, g/1000 kcal

	Ancestral diet	Recipe
Total fat	49	50
Saturated fats	15-20	19
Monounsaturated fats	15-25	20
Polyunsaturated fats	5-15	6
LA, omega-6	3.5-12	3.8
ALA, omega-3	1-4	1.1
LA/ALA	2:1 to 7:1	3.6:1
EPA + DHA	0.2–1	0.3
Overall omega-6/omega-3 ratio	2:1 to 6:1	3:1

Step 6. Review vitamins E and D
The last step is to review the vitamin D and E content of the diet. As I discussed in the last chapter, the amount of vitamin E needed is dependent upon the polyunsaturated fat content of the diet; the more PUFAs, the more vitamin E is required in the diet. This is a low PUFA diet, so the vitamin E requirements are not increased. With the poultry recipe we'll see how high PUFA content significantly increases the need for vitamin E. As Table 6.7 shows, this recipe meets vitamin D and E recommendations for puppies and adults. It meets recommended levels of vitamin D because it includes sardines and liver. Without both of these foods, vitamin D will probably be short. The recipe, with the spinach, meets recommended levels of vitamin E for adults and puppies.

Putting it all together
Our Recipe #1 contains 4,000 kcal, is high in protein, contains balanced, complete-and-defended fats, and complete-and-balanced minerals and vitamins, meeting NRC recommendations for all dogs, including pregnant or lactating bitches and puppies. This recipe will feed a typical adult 25-pound dog for one week. See Table 6.8 for feeding guidelines.

Let's take a complete look at the nutrient analyses of our beef recipe and see how nearly we approximated the ancestral diet. Table 6.5 shows that the relative levels of protein, fat, and carbohydrate are similar to the ancestral diet.

Table 6.5 Percentage protein, fat, and carbohydrate in beef recipe compared with ancestral diet

	Recipe, % calories	Ancestral, % calories
Protein	50	49
Fat	45	44
Carbohydrate	5	6

Next, we balanced the fats, per Table 6.6, making the fat profile similar to the ancestral diet.

Table 6.6 fats grams/1000 kcal

	Ancestral diet	Recipe
Total fat	49	50
Saturated fats	15-20	17
Monounsaturated fats	15-25	17
Polyunsaturated fats	5-15	6
LA, omega-6	3.5–12	3.8
ALA, omega-3	1-4	1.1
LA/ALA	2:1 to 7:1	3.6:1
EPA + DHA	0.2-1	0.3
Overall omega-6/omega-3 ratio	2:1 to 6:1	3:1

Finally, we completed the nutrition (vitamins and minerals) by adding fresh, whole foods as shown in Table 6.7.

Table 6.7 Recipe nutrient content compared with NRC and ancestral, per 1000 kcal

	Unit	NRC adult	NRC puppy	Ances-tral	Recipe
Minerals					
Ca	g	1.0	3.0	6.2	3.6
P	g	0.75	2.5	3.6	2.8
K	g	1.0	1.1	2.0	2.9
Na	g	0.2	0.55	1.0	1.4
Mg	g	0.15	0.10	0.4	0.29
Fe	mg	7.5	22	43	22
Cu	mg	1.5	2.7	6.0	3.9
Mn	mg	1.2	1.4	3.1	1.4
Zn	mg	15	25	24.5	28
I	mg	0.22	0.22		0.23
Se	mg	0.09	0.09	0.5	0.12
Vitamins					
A	IU	1137	1137	15375	16634
D	IU	136	136		138
E	IU	11.3	11.3	23	11
Thiamine	mg	0.56	0.34		0.62
Riboflavin	mg	1.30	1.32		2.8
Pantothenic Acid	mg	3.75	3.75		7.4
Niacin	mg	4.25	4.25		38.8
B6 (Pyridoxine)	mg	0.38	0.38		2.8
Folate	mg	0.068	0.068		0.3
B12	mg	0.01	0.01		0.04

Feeding amounts depend upon many factors, including your dog's activity level and outdoor temperatures. Use this chart as a starting point for determining how much of this recipe to feed.

Table 6.8 Feeding guidelines, ounces per day, 36 kcal per ounce

Dog's weight (pounds)	5	15	25	50	75	100
older, sleeps all day	4	8	12	21	28	35
adult, not active	4	10	15	25	33	41
moderate activity	5	12	17	28	38	48
active	6	14	20	34	45	56
very active	8	19	28	48	65	80
lactating moms	7	16	23	39	52	65
puppies						
young, <50% of adult wt	12	27	40	67	91	113
50–80% adult wt	10	22	32	54	73	90
80%+ adult wt	7	16	24	40	55	68

Recipe #2: Poultry

    2 pounds chicken necks, including bones (fat and skin removed)
    2 pounds chicken thighs (bone, fat and skin removed)
    ½ pound chicken hearts
    ½ pound chicken livers, preferably organic
    ½ pound yams
    ½ pound broccoli stalks
    ¼ pound oysters
    ¼ teaspoon kelp
    1 egg
    2 ounces freshly ground flaxseeds
    2 drops (40 IU) vitamin E
    1 ounce coconut oil

This 3,700 kcal recipe will feed a typical 20 to 25-pound adult dog for one week, and a 45-pound dog for three to four days. This recipe includes ground bones so we won't need to add sources of calcium and phosphorus as we did in the previous recipe. That means the bones must be fed raw, not lightly cooked. Cooked bones, unless very finely ground, can be dangerous for dogs because they are sharp and easily splinter.

Step 1. Choose lean meats

- *Two pounds of chicken necks or backs with skin and fat removed, or turkey necks without skin.*
- *Two pounds of lean thighs.*
- *One pound of livers and hearts.*

The lean meats in this recipe come from three sources: (1) necks or backs; (2) thighs; and (3) liver and heart. Instead of chicken, you can use turkey, duck, or pheasant.

Start with the necks or backs (including the bones) by removing all the external fat and skin. The skinned necks account for 40% of the meat used in the recipe and are 17% protein and 5.5% fat.

Many raw feeders feed chicken necks and backs because the prices are lower than most other parts of the chicken and the bones contain calcium and phosphorus. The necks and backs can be served ground or whole. While I give the necks whole to my dogs, I often advise people to feed the necks ground. Here's why: I start feeding my puppies raw, whole necks when they are three weeks old. They learn how to eat them and the whole necks become natural foods for them. On the other hand, some dogs, introduced to whole necks when they are adults, gulp the necks down. Many highly respected veterinarians, including some raw-feeding advocates, do not recommend giving whole raw bones to dogs, because there is a small risk that they could choke. My advice: grind the raw bones, unless your dog was introduced to whole raw bones at a very young age. Ask your butcher to grind the bones or, if you feed a lot of dogs or large dogs, buy a grinder.

The boneless thighs or legs count for the next 40% of the meat used in this recipe. Remove the storage fat (clumps of fat under the skin and throughout the body), but leave the thin fat strands within the muscle meat. The fat within the muscle meat, especially the dark meat, contains more long-chain polyunsaturated fats (including DHA) than the separable fats. This is what we want because the separated fats contain no DHA. With all the clumps of fat removed, chicken thighs are 20% protein and 4% fat.

The final 20% of meat is from organs. Add one half-pound of chicken hearts and one half-pound of chicken livers. You can use more hearts and fewer livers, but not more livers and fewer hearts. Livers are rich in vitamin A and too much can be harmful. These organs are mineral-rich and a favored part of the dog's ancestral diet.

I recommend using very lean meats in the chicken recipe because we're going to add more fat and carbohydrates. The chicken recipe contains ingredients such as eggs, omega-3 fats, and vegetables, which will decrease the caloric contribution of protein. At this point in the recipe, 60% of the calories come from protein, with our goal being 49%. We have a lot of room to add lower-protein ingredients and still have a high protein food.

Step 2. Ensure proper Ca and P range

With the boneless ruminant Recipe #1, we balanced the fats before we ensured the proper amounts of Ca and P, which we added with bonemeal. For bone-in poultry recipes, the bones are the primary source of Ca and P. It's best, therefore, to make sure that the recipe is within the proper Ca and P range before examining the fats. Table 6.9 shows that the Ca and P content of our recipe at this stage are similar to ancestral levels, and on the high side of NRC recommendations. This is what we want because we're going to add other foods that contain little or no Ca and P, thereby decreasing the overall Ca and P content.

Table 6.9 Ca and P, chicken recipe, meat only, g/1000 kcal

	Ca	P	Ca:P
NRC puppy	3	2.5	1.2:1
NRC adult	1	0.75	1.3:1
Ancestral	5.7	3.3	1.7:1
Recipe	5.1	3.8	1.3:1

Step 3. Add an egg, then balance, and complete the fats

- *Add one large egg, without the shell.*
- *Add 56 grams (2 ounces) of freshly ground flaxseeds.*

Eggs were part of the ancestral diet, and provided a wide range of important fats and other nutrients. Keeping poultry foods together, I usually add eggs to the chicken based diets only. For more information and suggestions on how to prepare eggs for dogs, see Chapter 4.

The egg in this recipe is 1.5% of the diet, slightly more than the egg percentage of the hypothetical ancestral diet. If you're rotating with the ruminant Recipe #1, the total egg content of the diet will be reduced to 0.75% of the diet.

I recommend you use regular commercial eggs. Omega-3 eggs will have different fat profiles and may be healthier than commercial eggs, but there is little reason to buy expensive omega-3 eggs for this recipe. We will add more omega-3s directly with flaxseeds or chia seeds and oysters.

After I add the eggs, I examine the balance of fats. Tables 6.10 and 6.11 show that at this stage—with just the meat and eggs—the recipe is still higher in protein and lower in carbohydrate and fat than our ideal, and that the fats are unbalanced. We'll first balance the fats, and then add carbohydrate with the vegetables. These steps will lower the protein right to where we want it to be. (Remember: protein + fat + carbohydrate = 100% of calories.)

Table 6.10 Percentage protein, fat, and carbohydrate (meat and eggs only) compared with ancestral diet

	Ancestral, % calories	Recipe, % calories
Protein	49	56
Fat	44	42
Carbohydrate	6	1.5

Table 6.11 Fatty acid profile with meat and egg, g/1000kcal

	Ancestral diet	Recipe
Total fat	49	44
Saturated fats	15-20	13
Monounsaturated fats	15-25	14
Polyunsaturated fats	5-15	11
LA, **omega-6**	3.5–12	8
ALA, omega-3	1-4	0.3*
LA/ALA	2:1 to 7:1	30:1*
EPA + DHA	0.2–1	0.6
Overall omega-6/omega-3 ratio	2:1 to 6:1	16:1*

does not meet standards

The fat profile in Table 6.11 shows that we need to add ALA (short-chain omega-3s) to the recipe, in order to balance the LA/ALA and overall omega-6/3 ratios. The recipe already meets our minimums for DHA because we are using lean poultry dark meat and removing all the separable fat. If we used chicken breasts instead of thighs the recipe would have about one-half the DHA content. While it's not essential that we add more DHA, I think it's advisable. We're going to add oysters, discussed below, to provide the additional DHA and a variety of trace minerals.

With chicken meats, the best oils to add are those rich in alpha-linolenic acid (ALA), a short-chain omega-3 fatty acid. Ground flaxseeds or chia seeds are the best sources of this. We do not want to add any other foods or oils high in linoleic acid including soybean, safflower, sunflower, canola, walnut, wheat germ, and hempseed oils.

Since we need manganese in this recipe, and flaxseed has about 50% more manganese than chia seeds, we'll use flaxseed in this recipe. In the next recipe, which contains other manganese-rich foods, we'll use chia seeds.

Table 6.12 shows that this recipe now has an excellent LA/ALA and overall omega-6/3 ratios, but at 14 grams is close to our recommended maximum (15 g) amount of polyunsaturated fat. That's always an issue with domesticated poultry, even with the use of the lean meats. We're going to reduce the PUFA percentage by adding other ingredients as shown in Steps 5 and 6.

Table 6.12 Fatty acid profile with meat, egg, oysters, and flaxseeds, g/1000 kcal

	Ancestral diet	Recipe
Total fat	49	47
Saturated fats	15-20	12
Monounsaturated fats	15-25	14
Polyunsaturated fats	5-15	14
LA, omega-6	3.5–12	8
ALA, omega-3	1-4	3.1
LA/ALA	2:1 to 7:1	2.7:1
EPA + DHA	0.2–1	0.7
Overall omega-6/omega-3 ratio	2:1 to 6:1	2.5:1

Step 4. Add vegetables and mineral-rich foods

- *One half pound of yams, one half pound broccoli stalks.*
- *One quarter pound of fresh oysters or one, 3.5-oz can oysters.*
- *One teaspoon high-iodine content kelp meal.*

Now we're going to add vegetables, fruits and other mineral-rich foods to balance and complete the minerals; add a variety of important antioxidants that help protect the brain and eyes; and add fiber. When feeding adult dogs lean chicken meats and organs, the only minerals we usually need to concern ourselves with are manganese, copper, and iodine. If we're feeding puppies, we also need to boost zinc.

Yams and broccoli stalks are both good sources of manganese. The yam will boost manganese levels enough to meet adult NRC recommendations, but when combined with brocoli stalks you will meet NRC puppy recommendations as well. Later, we will add kelp, which also contains manganese.

Oysters are a great source of copper and zinc for dogs. Zinc is a must for pregnant bitches. You can choose between fresh and canned oysters (but avoid those canned in China). The oysters also give the recipe a second source of vitamin D. With the oysters, the recipe now meets all NRC trace mineral recommendations for puppies and adults, with the exception of iodine, which we'll add below. An alternative to oysters is ¼ pound of beef liver, or commercial supplements of copper and zinc (5 mg of copper, 25 mg of zinc).

The amount of iodine in the oysters and the liver may be sufficient for this recipe, but I don't have reliable enough data to know for sure. To be safe, add one teaspoon of iodized salt or one quarter teaspoon high-iodine content kelp meal. I'm using the kelp that is 0.06% iodine in this analysis; one quarter teaspoon provides 600 mcg of iodine. Kelp also provides additional manganese, bringing this recipe closer to the ancestral diet.

The recipe now meets NRC mineral puppy recommendations, and approximates our ideal, the ancestral diet, as shown in Table 6.13.

Table 6.13 Mineral analysis, after vegetables and mineral rich foods, per 1000 kcal

Mineral	Unit	NRC adult	NRC puppy	Ancestral	Recipe
Ca	g	1.0	3.0	5.7	4.2
P	g	0.75	2.5	3.3	3.3
K	g	1.0	1.1	2.0	2.3
Na	g	0.2	0.55	1.0	0.65
Mg	g	0.15	0.10	0.4	0.33
Fe	mg	7.5	22	43	23
Cu	mg	1.5	2.7	6	2.8
Mn	mg	1.2	1.4	3.1	2.2
Zn	mg	15	25	24	47
I	mg	0.22	0.22		0.4
Se	mg	0.09	0.09	0.5	0.13

Step 5. Review the fats

> • *Add one ounce of coconut oil (not coconut milk).*

Coconut oil contains primarily saturated fats, including short and medium chain saturated fats, which are not available in poultry or ruminant fats, which have mostly long chain saturated fats. Coconut oil contains caprylic, capric and lauric acid, often called medium-chain triglycerides, which have been shown to have anti-microbial properties and other health benefits. Coconut oil also contains tocotrienols, an important vitamin E compound that is often not available in meat plus vegetable diets. Adding 1 oz of coconut oil increases the fat contribution to 47 grams per 1,000 kcal and 43% of calories and while reducing the protein content to 123 grams per 1,000 kcal—closer to the ancestral amount.

The addition of vegetables changed our fat level, so we need to ensure it is still in the ideal range. Table 6.14 shows the fat balance at this point.

Table 6.14 Fatty acid profile with meat, egg, vegetables, mineral-rich foods, g/1000 kcal

	Ancestral diet	Recipe
Total fat	49	43
Saturated fats	15-20	11
Monounsaturated fats	15-25	15
Polyunsaturated fats	5-15	13
LA, omega-6	3.5–12	8
ALA, omega-3	1-4	2.9
LA/ALA	2:1 to 7:1	2.7:1
EPA + DHA	0.2–1	0.7
Overall omega-6/omega-3 ratio	2:1 to 6:1	2.7:1

The recipe has 43 grams of fat and 130 grams of protein per 1000 kcal. This is higher in protein and lower in fat than our ideal, so we need to add some fat, but not polyunsaturated fats, because the 13 grams of PUFA /1000 kcal are getting close to the upper part of the range for PUFA, 5–15g/1000 kcal.

Step 6. Review vitamins D and E

- *Add two drops (usually 20 IUs per drop) of a high quality, naturally sourced, full-spectrum vitamin E.*

There is no need to add vitamin D to this recipe as it contains two vitamin D sources—oysters and livers. These two ingredients will probably provide enough vitamin D to meet recommendations.

Compared with beef, chicken has much higher levels of polyunsaturated fats (PUFAs), and therefore requires higher levels of antioxidant protection. As I discussed above, the more PUFAs, the more vitamin E is needed.

This recipe, with 13 grams of PUFAs per 1,000 kcal, is short vitamin E. The entire recipe should have 39 IUs to meet NRC recommendations, plus 33 IUs to compensate for the high PUFA content. The recipe has, according to the limited USDA data on vitamin E content of foods, 28 IUs, so we need to add 44 IUs of vitamin E to be sure the recipes meet vitamin E recommendations. To defend the fats, I normally prefer to add vitamin E rich foods, rather than synthesized supplements. That's one reason why I usually recommend flaxseed, which is loaded with antioxidants, rather than flaxseed oil; and sardines, also loaded with a variety of antioxidants, rather than salmon oil. But chicken-based foods already have a high LA omega-6 content and adding most natural sources of vitamin E, including almonds, walnuts, and sunflower seeds, can increase the total PUFAs above desired amounts.

Putting it all together

Recipe #2 feeds a typical 25-pound dog for one week. See Table 6.18 for feeding guidelines for all dogs.

Let's take a look at the nutrient analysis of our chicken recipe and see how nearly we approximated the ancestral diet. First, we used lean parts so that the amount of protein, fat, and carbohydrate are similar to the ancestral diet, Table 6.15.

Table 6.15 Percentage protein, fat, and carbohydrate, completed chicken recipe compared with ancestral diet

	Ancestral, % calories	Recipe, % calories
Protein	49	49
Fat	44	43
Carbohydrate	6	8

Next, we balanced the fats, Table 6.16.

Table 6.16 Recipe fat profile compared with ancestral diet, g/1000 kcal

	Ancestral diet	Recipe
Total fat	49	48
Saturated fats	15-20	17
Monounsaturated fats	15-25	15
Polyunsaturated fats	5-15	13
LA, omega-6	3.5–12	7
ALA, omega-3	1-4	2.7
LA/ALA	2:1 to 7:1	2.7:1
EPA + DHA	0.2–1	0.7
Overall omega-6/omega-3 ratio	2:1 to 6:1	2.6:1

Finally, we completed the nutrition (vitamins and minerals) by adding fresh, whole foods, Table 6.17.

Table 6.17 Recipe nutrient content compared with NRC and ancestral, per 1000 kcal

		NRC adult	NRC puppy	Ancestral	Recipe
Minerals					
Ca	g	1.0	3.0	5.7	3.9
P	g	0.75	2.5	3.3	3.0
K	g	1.0	1.1	2.0	2.2
Na	g	0.2	0.55	1.0	0.61
Mg	g	0.15	0.10	0.4	0.31
Fe	mg	7.5	22	43	22
Cu	mg	1.5	2.7	6	2.7
Mn	mg	1.2	1.4	3.1	1.7
Zn	mg	15	25	24	43
I	mg	0.22	0.22		0.3
Se	mg	0.09	0.09	0.5	0.12
Vitamins					
A	IU	1263	1263	15375	7867
D	IU	136	136		112
E	IU	11.3	11.3	23	41
Thiamine	mg	0.56	0.34		0.80
Riboflavin	mg	1.30	1.32		2.83
Pantothenic Acid	mg	3.75	3.75		12.3
Niacin	mg	4.25	4.25		36.5
B6 (Pyridoxine)	mg	0.38	0.38		2.8
Folate	mg	0.068	0.068		2.8
B12	mg	0.01	0.01		0.24
Choline	mg	425	425		514

Feeding amounts depend upon many factors, including your dog's activity level and outdoor temperatures. Use Table 6.18 as a starting point for determining how much of this recipe to feed.

Table 6.18 Feeding guidelines, ounces per day, 35 kcal per ounce

Dog's weight (pounds)	5	15	25	50	75	100
older, sleeps all day	4	9	13	21	28	35
adult, not active	4	10	15	25	33	41
moderate activity	5	12	17	28	38	48
active	6	14	20	34	45	56
very active	9	19	28	48	65	80
lactating moms	7	16	23	39	52	65
puppies						
young, <50% of adult wt	13	27	40	67	91	113
50–80% adult wt	10	22	32	54	73	90
80%+ adult wt	8	16	24	40	55	68

Rotating the two recipes

Rotating these two recipes is ideal, and improves the overall balance of fat from very good to excellent. One week feed the beef/ruminant recipe and the next week the poultry recipe. If you can, rotate the ruminants (beef, lamb, bison, venison) and poultry (chicken, turkey, pheasant, and duck) and serve a variety of colorful vegetables and fruits with them.

Let's look at the overall nutrition of rotating ruminant and poultry recipes as shown in tables 6.19, 6.20, and 6.21.

Table 6.19 Fatty acid profiles, g/1000 kcal

	Ancestral diet	ABC beef	ABC chicken	Rotated
Total fat	49	50	48	49
Saturated fats	15-20	17	17	17
Monounsaturated fats	15-25	17	15	16
Polyunsaturated fats	5-15	6	13	9
LA, omega-6	3.5-12	3.8	7	5
ALA, omega-3	1-4	1.1	2.7	1.8
LA/ALA	2:1 to 7:1	3.6:1	2.7:1	3:1
EPA + DHA	0.2–1	0.3	0.7	0.6
Overall omega-6/ omega-3 ratio	2:1 to 6:1	3.1:1	2.6:1	2.6:1

Table 6.20 Combined recipes, compared with NRC and ancestral, per 1000 kcal

	Unit	NRC adult	NRC puppy	Ancestral	Recipe
Minerals					
Ca	g	1.0	3.0	5.7	3.6
P	g	0.75	2.5	3.3	2.8
K	g	1.0	1.1	2.0	2.5
Na	g	0.2	0.55	1.0	0.98
Mg	g	0.15	0.10	0.4	0.29
Fe	mg	7.5	22	43	33
Cu	mg	1.5	2.7	6	3.1
Mn	mg	1.2	1.4	3.1	1.5
Zn	mg	15	25	24	34
I	mg	0.22	0.22		0.3
Se	mg	0.09	0.09	0.5	0.12
Vitamins					
A	IU	1263	1263	15375	11980
D	IU	136	136		125
E	IU	11.3	11.3	23	125
Thiamine	mg	0.56	0.34		0.69
Riboflavin	mg	1.30	1.32		2.72
Pantothenic Acid	mg	3.75	3.75		9.5
Niacin	mg	4.25	4.25		36.3
B6 (Pyridoxine)	mg	0.38	0.38		2.7
Folate	mg	0.068	0.068		0.27
B12	mg	0.01	0.01		0.025
Choline	mg	425	425		553

Recipe #3: The perfect fat and protein recipe

Here are two variations of what I call the "perfect fat and protein" recipe: the first is designed for puppies and pregnant bitches (although it would work for any dog); and the second for adult dogs only. I use specific, mineral-rich vegetables for the puppy recipes, although the less demanding adult recipes can use almost any vegetables. These recipes contain the ancestral amounts and balance of well defended-from-oxidation fats, protein, and carbohydrate. Since these diets contain ground bone, they are best served raw. Both recipes will feed a typical 25-pound adult dog for one week.

In order to produce a perfect fat balance, I use two sources of meat in this recipe: beef and chicken. If you want to feed just one animal source at a time, which I normally recommend, stick to rotating Recipes 1 and 2. If, on the other hand, there are times when you want to make just one recipe, for example, if you're having a dog sitter feed your dogs for a few weeks, this recipe may be ideal.

Perfect fat and protein recipe for puppies: 3,930 kcal

2¼ pounds 93% lean beef
1¾ pounds chicken necks, skin and fat removed
½ pound beef heart
½ pound beef liver
½ pound canned pumpkin
½ pound cooked oat bran*
¼ pound Swiss chard
¼ pound broccoli stalks
¼ pound US oysters
1 (3.75 oz) can of sardines in water
2 ounces freshly ground chia seeds
1 egg
2 teaspoons coconut oil (8 grams)
1 teaspoon iodized salt
2 drops (20 IUs per drop) naturally sourced vitamin E

Perfect fat and protein recipe for adults: 3,800 kcal
2¼ pounds 90–93% lean beef
1¾ pounds chicken necks, skin and fat removed
1 pounds mixed, colorful vegetables and fruits
½ pound beef heart
½ pound beef liver
½ pound cooked oat bran*
1 (3.75 oz) can of sardines in water
2 ounces freshly ground chia or flaxseeds
1 egg
2 teaspoons coconut oil
2 teaspoons iodized salt
2 drops (20 IU) natural sourced vitamin E

*Dogs who have allergies to wheat should not be fed oats. For these dogs, and for those people wanting to feed grain-free recipes, replace the oat bran with an additional ½ pound of sweet potato or canned pumpkin, plus 1 pound of vegetables or fruit (for fiber and carbohydrate), and replace the iodized salt with ½ teaspoon high-mineral content kelp.

Ingredient analysis
Meats. Feed 93% lean meats to pregnant and lactating bitches and young puppies, and 90% lean for adults. Some Dalmatians and Bedlington Terriers may require low copper diets—if yours is one of these, use chicken livers instead of beef livers. Beef liver, according to USDA data, has ten times the copper content of chicken livers. Ask your veterinarian or your dog's breeder for advice about the copper needs of your dog.

Vegetables. Most of the minerals and vitamins in these recipes come from the meats and seafoods, with the exception of manganese. For adult dogs, I'm not using vegetables for their mineral content, so you can feed the vegetables and fruits that are left over from what you eat. For puppies, you should feed mineral-rich vegetables. (See Chapter 4 for a list of vegetables not to feed.)

Fats. To balance the short chain omega-6s and -3s, I recommend two ounces of freshly ground chia seeds. You can find chia seeds online—most stores don't carry them. You can use flaxseeds instead, but if you also feed the chicken recipe (#2 above) I prefer to use chia seeds in this recipe. For EPA and DHA, the long chain omega-3s, I add one (3.75 oz) can of sardines (in water, no salt added) and ¼ pound U.S.A. oysters (not from China), for the zinc and fatty acids. It is okay to add two cans of sardines and no oysters for adults, but for young puppies and pregnant and lactating bitches I recommend keeping the oysters for the added zinc. If your dog has "fish breath," you can reduce the seafood by 50%, still meet all adult dog standards, and have a good fatty acid balance.

I've added two teaspoons of coconut oil for the short chain saturated fats, and to increase the overall fat content. Lightly warm the coconut oil for better mixing.

Egg. For advice on proper preparation of eggs, see Chapter 4.

Oat bran. Even though oat bran, a grain, is not a natural food for dogs and is not part of their ancestral diet, it is a healthy food for most dogs. Oat bran is an excellent source of manganese and fiber, and increases the carbohydrate content of our recipe to 6% of calories, similar to the ancestral diet. Oats, a low-gluten grain, are tolerated well by most dogs, except those who have wheat allergies and gluten intolerances. Glutens are proteins in grains, especially wheat, that cause the elastic texture of dough. A small percentage of dogs cannot tolerate gluten (celiac disease), and should avoid high gluten containing grains, especially wheat, rye, and barley.

Vitamin E. Rather than the 40 IUs (usually two drops) of refined vitamin E, you can add two teaspoons of wheatgerm oil, or two ounces freshly ground almonds or walnuts. The nuts and wheatgerm oil add polyunsaturated fats, which will throw off the perfect fat balance in this recipe, but it will still be in the acceptable range.

Nutrient analysis

Let's take a look at the nutrient analysis of our perfect fat recipe and see how nearly we have approximated the ancestral diet. First, we use lean meats so that the amount of protein, fat, and carbohydrate are similar to the ancestral diet, Table 6.21.

Table 6.21 Protein, fat, carbohydrate contributions—as close to the ancestral diet as one can get

	Ancestral, g/1000 kcal	Recipe, g/1000 kcal	Recipe, % calories
Protein	123	124	49
Fat	49	49	44
Carbohydrate	16	16	6

Next, we balance the fats, Table 6.22.

Table 6.22 The perfect fatty acid profile. PUFAs right in the middle of the ancestral range, ample DHA, all in natural, highly absorbable forms, ideal omega-6 to omega-3 ratio, g/1000 kcal

	Ancestral diet	Recipe
Total fat	49	49
Saturated fats	15-20	17
Monounsaturated fats	15–25	17
Polyunsaturated fats	5–15	9
LA, omega-6	3.5–12	4.8
ALA, omega-3	1-4	2.3
LA/ALA	2:1 to 7:1	2.1:1
EPA + DHA	0.2–1	0.6
Overall omega-6/omega-3 ratio	2:1 to 6:1	2:1

Finally, we complete the nutrition (vitamins and minerals) by adding fresh, whole foods, Table 6.23.

Table 6.23 Vitamin and minerals of recipe compared with NRC and ancestral, g/1000 kcal

	Unit	NRC adult	NRC puppy	Ancestral	Recipe
Minerals					
Ca	g	1.0	3.0	5.7	3.3
P	g	0.75	2.5	3.3	2.8
K	g	1.0	1.1	2.0	2.1
Mg	g	0.2	0.55	1.0	1.0
Fe	g	0.15	0.10	0.4	0.26
Cu	mg	7.5	22	43.1	22
Mn	mg	1.20	1.4	3.1	1,6
Zn	mg	15	25	24	34
I	mg	0.22	0.22		0.23
Se	mg	0.09	0.09	0.5	0.14
Vitamins					
A	IU	1263	1263	15375	21010
D	IU	136	136		141
E	IU	7.5	7.5	23	15
Thiamine	mg	0.56	0.34		0.7
Riboflavin	mg	1.30	1.32		3.2
Pantothenic Acid	mg	3.75	3.75		10
Niacin	mg	4.25	4.25		36
B6 (Pyridoxine)	mg	0.38	0.38		2.5
Folate	mg	0.068	0.068		0.09
B12	mg	0.01	0.01		0.05
Choline	mg	425	425		626

Feeding amounts depend upon many factors, including your dog's activity level and outdoor temperatures. Use this chart as a starting point for determining how much of this recipe to feed.

Table 6.24 Feeding guidelines, ounces per day, perfect fat recipe. This recipe has 34 kcal ME per ounce; the total recipe contains 3,850 kcal

Weight of dog (pounds)	5	15	25	50	75	100
older, sleeps all day	4	9	13	22	30	37
adult, not active	5	11	15	26	35	44
moderate activity	5	12	18	30	41	51
active	6	14	21	36	48	60
very active	9	20	30	51	69	85
lactating moms	7	17	24	41	56	69
puppies						
young, <50% of adult wt	13	29	42	71	96	120
50–80% of adult wt	10	23	34	57	78	96
80%+ adult wt	8	17	25	43	58	72

Chapter 7

STORING FOODS TO RETAIN QUALITY

HOW YOU STORE DRY AND FROZEN FOODS MAKES A HUGE DIFFERENCE

One of the most popular parts of my seminars is the discussion of proper storage of dry and frozen foods. It makes no sense to buy expensive, premium dog foods, whether dry or frozen, and then ruin them—actually making them unhealthy—by storing them too long or improperly. Recently produced, mass-market food is probably better than super-premium, top-of-the-line foods that have sat on the shelf for months. Here's some important advice on ensuring the foods you buy are at their best when you feed them.

Dry foods: Buy recently produced and use up within 14 days after opening.

Would you keep a loaf of bread open in your kitchen or garage for 39 days? I hope not. That's how long the typical purchased bag of dog food remains open before completely consumed. This lengthy shelf time, combined with often poor storage conditions, leads to oxidation of fats, nutrient degradation, and infestation by molds, mites, and other food spoilers. One in three dogs dies of cancer, and I think improper storage at home is a contributing factor.

Dry dog foods usually have a one-year "shelf life." That means the food is "good" for up to one year after the manufacturing date. Many dry foods stamp a "best if used by" date on the package. This applies only to *unopened* bags.

If the bag is intact, without any holes or tears, not enough oxygen can migrate into the food in one year to cause significant oxidation, nutrient degradation, or microbial growth problems. *But as soon as you open the bag of dog food,* oxygen, moisture, light, mold spores, storage mites, and other potential spoilers enter the bag.

Oxidation of fats. Dog food companies use antioxidants (sometimes vitamin E and other natural sources) to forestall oxidation. Over time, with continual exposure to oxygen whenever you open the bag (and the bags are not perfect oxygen barriers either), the antioxidants are eventually all oxidized (used up) and the fats, beginning with the more fragile omega-3s, start turning rancid. As discussed above, studies show that frequent consumption of oxidized fats may cause cancer and contribute to many chronic health problems.[41]

Degradation of all micronutrients. The nutrition in the food at the bottom of a bag left open 39 days will be considerably reduced compared to that of the top of the bag. Vitamins particularly susceptible to loss of potency due to long-term room temperature storage include vitamin A, thiamin, most forms of folate, some forms of vitamin B6 (pyridoxal), vitamin C, and pantothenic acid.

Molds and mycotoxins. Storing open bags of dry dog food for 39 days in warm, humid areas (most kitchens) promotes the growth of molds. Some of the waste products of these molds (mycotoxins) are increasingly being implicated as long-term causes of cancer and other health problems in humans, poultry, pigs, and other animals. Dogs are particularly susceptible to these toxins.[42]

When dry dog foods absorb moisture from the surrounding air, the antimicrobials used by manufacturers to delay mold growth can be overwhelmed, and mold can grow.[43] The molds that consume dry pet foods include the Aspergillus flavus mold, which produces Aflatoxin B1, the most potent naturally occurring carcinogenic substance known.

People can't see low levels of mold with the naked eye, and most dogs can't taste it.[44] While some dogs have died shortly after eating mycotoxin-contaminated foods, mycotoxins kill most dogs slowly by suppressing the immune system and creating long-term health problems in all organs of the body.[45, 46] This topic is covered at length in *See Spot Live Longer*.

Infestation. Bugs, storage mites, mice, and other unpleasant invaders thrive on dry dog food. Recent research has shown that allergic dogs frequently have reactions to the carcasses of storage mites. Storage mites may infest grains, especially those grains used in low cost dry dog foods.

Strategies to enhance storage life of dry food
Here are my recommendations:

1. Keep food in its original bag, even if you use an airtight container. Pouring the food out exposes all the pieces of kibble to air, increasing the potential for oxidation.

2. Buy small, recently produced, bags of food. Look for manufacturing or "best if used by" dates on the bag. If you don't see one, ask the retailer for the date. If you can't understand the code, ask the retailer to interpret it for you.

3. Once opened, plan to have food consumed within 7 days.

4. Keep food dry. If the food looks moist, throw it away.

5. Keep larger bags in the freezer.

6. If the food has changed color, throw it away.

7. If the food smells rancid or like paint, throw it away.

8. If your dog refuses to eat at mealtime, do not force her to eat.

9. Don't buy bags that are torn.

These storage strategies are based upon an article written by Steve Brown and Beth Taylor, originally published on www.mercola.com.

The shelf life of commercial raw diets: three months

If you are feeding commercially prepared raw foods, it's important to buy recently produced frozen foods. Even if the meats and vegetables are all organic and the fats perfectly balanced, it is not a "quality" product, by USDA definition, if it is older than four months old. I'd prefer even fresher food.

Freezing is the best way to preserve meats, but the nutrients in the meat still degrade and the fats oxidize, even at 0 degrees F. Whole frozen meats have up to a one year "shelf life" in the freezer. However, ground meats—the number one ingredient in almost all commercial frozen raw diets—have a much shorter shelf life.

According to the USDA, ground meats, to be considered quality, have 3 to 4 month shelf lives when frozen. Here is a portion of the USDA frozen storage chart, based on frozen meats kept at a constant 0 degrees F (-18 degrees C).[47]

Item	Months
Meat, uncooked roasts	4 to 12
Meat, uncooked steaks or chops	4 to 12
Meat, uncooked ground	3 to 4
Poultry, uncooked whole	12
Poultry, uncooked parts	9
Poultry, uncooked giblets	3 to 4

Grinding meats break the protective cell walls of the meat and fat cells, making the fragile nutrients more exposed to oxidizing agents, including the copper and iron released by the broken cells. These metals speed up the oxidation process.

Once the ground meat is frozen, oxidation and destruction of nutrients does not stop. Unless the food is packaged in glass or metal and is never opened, oxygen migrates into the food and oxidation occurs. The fats slowly turn rancid and the vitamins and antioxidants slowly degrade. The nutrients are further damaged by the growth of ice crystals. When raw meat freezes, the water within the meat forms ice crystals; the ice crystals grow even at a steady 0 degrees F. The longer the time in the freezer, the larger the ice crystals become, and the more likely that they will further puncture cell walls, and break some of the double bonds in the polyunsaturated fats.

The way most raw diets are made—using ground meats mixed with vegetables and other nutrients—can accelerate degradation of nutrients, and shortens the shelf life. Ground vegetables are mostly water, which, when frozen, form more ice crystals, further damaging nutrients. Added fish oils shorten shelf lives further because the ice crystals can break some of the double bonds of the polyunsaturated fats. Ground fish products have the shortest shelf lives of all animal protein.

The best way to ensure that you are buying a quality (by USDA definition) product, is to look for the "produced-on date," and then buy only products that are less than three months old. Many raw diet manufacturers give their products 12-month shelf lives (I did at my company, Steve's Real Food, until I learned better), and place "best if used by" dates on their labels. In retrospect, this was not good enough as the buyer needs to know when it was produced. If you can't make that determination from the packaging, contact the manufacturer or ask your retailer how to determine when the product was produced. Demand freshness.

Chapter 8

ADVANCED NUTRITIONAL CONCEPTS

This chapter is designed for those who want additional information on some of the materials presented in the first seven chapters. For many of you, this information is over and above what you need to know to feed the ABC way. For those of you want this level of information, the concepts and research to be covered here include:

1. An introduction to the chemistry of fats for dogs.

2. Do wild prey animals produce different fats than domesticated animals?

3. Dogs and carbohydrates.

4. Kidneys and high protein diets.

5. Pet food math.

An introduction to the chemistry of fats for dogs

As discussed throughout the book, the issue of fats in a dog's diet—both the amount and balance—is important and not well understood by most dog owners. Fortunately, by following the recommendations in the previous chapters, it's easy to improve the fat balance and add defended-from-oxidation DHA and other essential fats, whether you're feeding dry, frozen, or homemade foods. If you want to know why I have made those recommendations, this section is for you. Follow me on this short journey into the chemistry of fats for dogs. It's exciting, because recent science shows that we can really help our dogs be smarter and healthier by improving the balance of fats we feed them.

The chemistry of fatty acids

The fats in our food consist primarily of fatty acids, which are chains of one to twenty-four carbon atoms with hydrogen atoms attached. In chemistry-speak, it looks a little like this: C-C-C-C-C-C-C-C-C-C-C-C, a 12-carbon saturated (all single bonds) fatty acid. All the carbon atoms, except the ones at each end of the chain, have hydrogen atoms attached all around then; the carbon atoms are *saturated* with hydrogen.

How the carbon atoms are attached to each other and the number of carbon atoms in the chain determines the type of fat and the properties of the fat. The carbon atoms can be attached to each other with single bonds, sharing one electron, or with double bonds, sharing two electrons. In chemistry-speak, it looks like this: C-C-C-C-C-C-C-C-C-C=C-C-C-C-C-C, a 16-carbon monounsaturated (mono = one double bond) fatty acid. Single bonds are more stable than double bonds; it's easier to share one electron than two. Fatty acids with only single bonds, saturated fats, are more stable—less likely to go rancid—than those with one or more double bonds, the monounsaturated and polyunsaturated fats.

There are three broad categories of fatty acids: saturated fatty acids (SFAs) with no double bonds; monounsaturated fatty acids (MUFAs) with one double bond; and polyunsaturated fatty acids (PUFAs) with more than one double bond. No fat is totally saturated or unsaturated. Almost all natural fat sources contain SFAs, MUFAs, and PUFAs, as shown in Table 8.2. Natural fats may contain 50 to 60 different fatty acids. For instance, cow's milk has at least 60 different fatty acids and most fish contain 50 or more different types of fat.

Saturated fatty acids

Saturated fatty acids have no double bonds; adjacent carbon atoms share only one electron. This is a stable relationship, and therefore saturated fats, like coconut oil and beef fat, do not readily oxidize and have long shelf lives. There are many types of saturated fats, depending upon how many carbon atoms are attached. The shorter the saturated fat (the fewer the number of carbon atoms), the more readily it burns, and the more easily the dog can digest it. Coconut oil is rich in short chain saturated fats, and animal fats are rich in the longer saturated fats.

Saturated fats provide flavor and energy, and assist in the absorption of fat-soluble vitamins. Some of the short-chain (2–6 carbon atoms) saturated fats are reported to have anti-microbial properties—which may help prevent some bacterial and viral diseases. Saturated fats are required in cell membranes. Too much saturated fat (which I define as more than 20 g/1,000 kcal or more than 20 grams per day for a 45-pound pet dog) can lead to health problems, including reducing the dog's ability to learn and remember.

Almost all fat-containing foods have some saturated fats. As long as there is enough fat in the diet, there's usually enough saturated fat.

Monounsaturated fatty acids
Monounsaturated fatty acids have one double bond; they are therefore more prone to going rancid than saturated fats. If packaged and handled well, they are shelf stable for several months or more, especially if they contain antioxidants. Most plant and animal fats contain MUFAs. Olive oil, avocado, nuts, and bone marrow having especially high MUFAs content. Monounsaturated fatty acids are also found in the cell membranes of plants and animals—their fluidity helps keep animals' arteries supple. Some reports indicate that too many MUFAs may interfere with the functions of the essential polyunsaturated fats. The ancestral diet contained 15–25 g/1,000 kcal of MUFAs and I think that is a wise target.

Polyunsaturated fatty acids
Polyunsaturated fatty acids have more than one double bond. Sharing two electrons (double bonds) is not a stable relationship; an oxygen atom can come along and take an electron, which oxidizes the fat. That's why polyunsaturated fats go rancid quickly when exposed to air and light, unless protected by a variety of antioxidants. The more double bonds (DHA has six) in a fatty acid, the more prone it is to rancidity.

Where the first double bond is determines the properties of the fat and whether it is an omega-6 or omega-3 fat, the two primary types of PUFAs. Because humans and dogs cannot make a double bond after the third carbon atom—omega-3 fatty acids (abbreviated n-3), and omega-6 fatty acids (n-6)—*it is therefore essential for dogs (and humans) to obtain these fatty acids from the diet; these are the essential fatty acids, or EFAs.* It is important that there are proper amounts of total PUFAs (5–15 g/1,000 kcal), the omega-6 and omega-3s are balanced in the range of 2:1 to 6:1, and that a complete range of n-6s and n-3s are included in the diet.

Omega-6 fatty acids

The four primary omega-6 fats are linoleic acid (LA), gamma linoleic acid (GLA), conjugated linolenic acid (CLA), and arachidonic acid (AA). LA is the simplest and most stable, and is used within the body primarily to make the longer chain omega-6 fatty acids, such as arachidonic acid. Depending upon its health and other factors, a dog can convert 18-carbon LA to GLA, CLA, and then to 20-carbon AA, the primary fat in the brain. It takes energy and special enzymes to make this conversion, so a dog under stress can have difficulties producing sufficient quantities of these "conditionally essential" (essential during times of high stress or growth) fatty acids. Lack of LA in the diet will cause the dog's coat to fall out, make the dog sluggish, or eventually kill the dog. Lack of AA, GLA, and CLA in the diet has more subtle effects; lack of AA, a brain fat, in a puppy's diets can produce a "dumber" adult dog. On the other hand, too much LA and AA can cause inflammation throughout the dog's body, and can crowd out the use of DHA in the dog's brain, again producing a dumber dog.

Omega-3 fatty acids

The three primary omega-3 fatty acids are ALA, EPA, and DHA. The simplest omega-3 is ALA (alpha linolenic acid), which we get from flaxseed, chia, hempseed, walnuts, and other plants. Humans and dogs use ALA primarily for the raw ingredients to make EPA and DHA, which are essential for optimal body, brain, and eye health. Most dogs can convert some (0.1–15%) of the 18-carbon ALA to the 20-carbon EPA and then to the 22-carbon DHA, but recent studies show that some dogs (including older dogs, young puppies, and adult dogs under stress) can't convert enough ALA to DHA to meet their needs and therefore need a dietary source of DHA, usually from fish or fish oils. Many dog foods contain ALA, which is less expensive and more stable than DHA, and tout their "omega-3s," but it's not the same: to be at their best physically and mentally, dogs need to consume defended-from-oxidation DHA.

The misleading omega-6 to omega-3 ratio

Many researchers recommend an omega-6 to -3 ratio of 2:1 to 7:1. Responding to consumer demands, many dog food manufacturers list the omega-6/-3 ratio on their packages or websites. A good omega-6 to omega-3 ratio, though, does not mean that the fats are balanced and complete.

Evaluating foods and diets based upon a listed omega-6/-3 ratio is often not helpful for two reasons.[49] First, a "perfect ratio" of omega-6/-3 of 3:1 is not a balanced fat diet for dogs if all the omega-3s are ALA from plant sources and do not include a source of defended-from-oxidation DHA. Second, the amounts of omega-6s and -3s are equally important as the ratio of omega-6s/-3s. As you can see in the Table 8.1 below, some diets (in this case 93% lean beef) have good omega-6/-3 ratios, but do not have enough omega-6s to meet minimum requirements, and therefore are not healthy. Similarly, some diets have good ratios, but contain too many PUFAs. Too few or too many omega-6s and -3s, even in the ideal ratio, may contribute to health problems, including premature aging.[50]

Table 8.1 93% lean beef, good ratio, but insufficient amounts of LA and ALA, g/1000 kcal

	Ancestral diet	93% lean beef
Total fat	49	49
Saturated fats	15-20	21
Monounsaturated fats	15-25	21
Polyunsaturated fats	5-15	2*
LA, omega-6	3.5-12	1.5*
ALA, omega-3	1-4	0.2
LA/ALA	2:1 to 7:1	6.5:1

does not meet standards

Table 8.2 Fatty acid content of various oils

	SFAs	MUFAs	PUFAs	Grams omega-6/kg	Grams omega-3/kg	Ratio -6/-3
Almond oil	9%	73%	18%	174	0	
Beef tallow	52%	44%	4%	33	5	6.6
Borage oil	14%	24%	61%	610	0	
Canola oil	7%	62%	31%	208	92	2.3
Chicken fat	31%	47%	22%	199	8	25
Coconut oil	92%	6%	2%	18	0	
Cod liver oil	25%	51%	25%	19	215	0.1
Corn oil	14%	29%	57%	536	12	45
Flaxseed oil	10%	21%	69%	127	558	0.2
Hempseed oil	11%	13%	75%	564	182	3.1
Olive oil	14%	75%	11%	98	7	14
Safflower oil	7%	78%	15%	144	0	
Salmon oil	22%	33%	45%	22	396	0.1
Soybean oil	17%	24%	59%	510	72	7.1
Sunflower oil	9%	60%	30%	289	0	
Walnut oil	10%	14%	76%	586	146	4.0

Defended fats

PUFAs are fragile. Increased consumption of PUFAs, especially DHA, EPA and AA, is healthful only if the fats are well defended-from-oxidation, before and after the dog consumes them.

One of the most important lessons I learned about formulating dog foods was: *what can oxidize will oxidize.* Many years ago I developed a freeze-dried "raw" food. Freeze drying removes the moisture in a food at low temperatures, thereby preserving most of the nutrients. I packaged the product in a high-barrier-to-oxygen foil bag, and included an oxygen scavenger (one of the small packets often found in vitamin jars) in the bag to absorb the oxygen left in the bag after packaging. Theoretically, I should have had a stable product, with a shelf life of at least one year. But when I tested the product every month for oxidizing fats, I found a steadily deteriorating product. The fats—probably EPA and DHA—were becoming rancid. The defenses against oxidation I utilized were not sufficient. It's not just the DHA and EPA in the food that will oxidize; these fats in the dog's cells can oxidize as well. I define *defended fats as those having enough defenses against oxidation to protect the fats before and after ingestion.*

Before ingestion, the fats need physical defenses such as eggshells, nutshells, fish scales, and opaque glass packages, and antioxidant protection to prevent them from going rancid. After ingestion, the fats must be protected by sufficient amounts of a variety of antioxidants obtained from the diet, including vitamin E and carotenes. Without sufficient antioxidant protection, for example, the DHA in the cell membranes of the dog's eyes may oxidize, and the dog may lose vision as she ages.

Do wild prey animals produce different fats than domesticated animals?

Hypothesis: Domesticated prey animals, even if they are fed the same food, will not have the same types of fat as wild prey animals because they don't need the same types of fats.

A wild animal needs to hear and see well, think and move quickly in order to survive. It needs significant amounts of DHA, a very fluid fat, to do these tasks well. Generally speaking, areas of the body that require rapid movement contain DHA (a hummingbird's wings are rich in DHA, for example). I suspect that wild prey animals will convert more of the ALA they consume (from grasses) to DHA than domesticated animals that have no need for rapid movement or alertness.

It's expensive—in terms of energy and nutrients—for an animal to convert ALA to DHA and then store the DHA. The domesticated pasture-fed animal has no need to convert the ALA it eats to DHA, so it probably won't make as much DHA as the wild animal. Why waste the energy converting ALA to DHA when it's not needed? DHA requires greater protection against oxidation than ALA, putting a further strain on the animal. When it comes to storing fat, saturated fats are much more stable.

A pasture-raised ruminant, with little need to think and move quickly, would probably store as much fat as possible as stable, saturated fats, and use much of the polyunsaturated fats it consumes for what minimal energy needs it has. The wild animal, with a greater need for the polyunsaturated fats, probably converts more of the saturated fats to energy. Fed the same foods (different quantities based upon activity levels), domesticated prey animals would therefore have more saturated fats, and a higher percentage of their polyunsaturated fats will be short-chain fats than with wild prey animals, who would have a higher percentage of long-chain polyunsaturated fats, particularly DHA.

Dogs and carbohydrates

Do dogs need carbohydrates? No, dogs do not need carbohydrates, as long as they are eating a high protein diet. All the leading canine nutrition textbooks, quoted below, agree. But that does not mean all dogs should not consume carbohydrates. Carbohydrates provide a significantly less expensive source of energy than protein and most fats. While, in a perfect world, I'd prefer for dogs to eat low carbohydrate diets, in the real world it is often essential for dogs to consume considerable amounts of carbohydrates to reduce the cost of the dog food for the dog's owner, and the cost of producing meat on the environment.

Moderate amounts (up to one-third by weight of the recipe) of high protein, mineral rich carbohydrates such as sweet potatoes, yams, and low gluten grains such as oats and rice, are healthy for most adult dogs, *as long as the fats in the recipe are balanced and the meats lean.* In Appendix A, I present four high protein, low-and-balanced fat, moderate-carbohydrate content recipes, developed in conjunction with Mary Straus, originally published in the *Whole Dog Journal.*

While some raw food "purists" may object to feeding any carbohydrates to dogs, I pose the following question:

Q. Which is healthier—very high levels of fats, or moderate levels of carbohydrates from nutrient rich foods, such as sweet potatoes?

A. I think a strong argument can be made that moderate levels of carbohydrates from nutrient rich sources are healthier for most adult dogs than diets high in saturated fats (typical raw beef products) or polyunsaturated fats (typical chicken products).

Here are comments from four of the leading textbooks about the role of carbohydrates in dog foods:

Canine and Feline Nutrition (co-authored by two scientists from Iams): "The fact that dogs and cats do not require carbohydrate is immaterial because the nutrient content of most commercial foods include (carbohydrates)."[51]

Small Animal Clinical Nutrition IV, published by the founder of Science Diet: "Dogs and cats do not have an absolute dietary requirement for carbohydrates in the same way that essential amino acids or fatty acids must be provided.... From a practical sense, the answer to this question is of little importance because there are carbohydrates in most food ingredients used in commercially prepared dog foods."[52]

The Waltham Book of Companion Animal Nutrition: "There is no known minimum dietary requirement for carbohydrate..."[53]

Nutrient Requirements of Dogs and Cats, from the National Research Council of the National Academies (NRC), 2006, states that even pregnant and lactating bitches do not need a dietary source of carbohydrate as long as they have a high protein diet.[54]

Is Carbohydrate a Dirty Word?

You won't find carbohydrates listed on your dog food bag even though almost all dog foods consist of at least some carbs. In the guaranteed analysis, required on every dog food or treat sold in the U.S., you'll find water, protein, fat, and fiber. The word "carbohydrate" is almost never mentioned. Fiber is an indigestible carbohydrate—it is primarily plant cell walls resistant to digestion.

Members of the Association of American Feed Control Officials (AAFCO) regulate pet foods, including treats and supplements, on a state-by-state basis. Manufacturers must send labels of all the pet foods they sell to the association member in each state, who then reviews the label and issues a license to allow sale of that product in the state. Most members follow the model regulations as designated by AAFCO. If a label does not follow AAFCO regulations, the state regulator may decide not to license the product. If the product is sold without a license, the regulator can go into a store and remove the product, which is not a good thing to happen to a pet food manufacturer. Therefore, most pet food companies play by AAFCO's rules (the more powerful companies help make the rules).

AAFCO guidelines, as published in the *Official Publication of the Association of American Feed Control Officials,* discourage the use of the word "carbohydrate" anywhere on a pet food label. Here are the exact words:

> "...carbohydrate guarantees are no longer considered as necessary or meaningful for purchaser information, therefore, their future use is discouraged."[55]

Technical manuals are not regulated by AAFCO, but one can still rarely find "carbohydrate" mentioned, whether the manual is written for veterinarians or dog guardians. For example, in a publication for veterinarians, *Applied Clinical Nutrition of the Dog and Cat, A Guide to Waltham Veterinary Diets,* the word "carbohydrate" is not even mentioned in the 44 page technical discussion of their Veterinary Canine Calorie Control Diet and Canine Restricted Protein Diets. Waltham lists protein, fat, ash, crude fiber content and 12 minerals, 11 vitamins, 11 amino acids, but not carbohydrates. [56]

Kidneys and high protein diets
There are many myths in the world of dog foods. One of them is that high protein diets damage the kidneys of dogs. Mary Straus, writing for the *Whole Dog Journal,* responds to this myth:

> *Research done on dogs has now proved that protein does not damage kidneys, and feeding a lower protein diet does not protect them. In fact, senior dogs fed high protein diets live longer and are healthier than those that are fed low protein diets, even when one kidney has been removed. Studies conducted at the University of Georgia in the 1990s demonstrated that feeding protein levels of 34 percent [on a dry matter basis] to older dogs with chronic kidney failure and dogs with only one kidney caused no ill effects.*

These same studies did raise the issue of whether low-protein diets may cause harm. The mortality rate was greater for the dogs fed 18 percent protein than for the ones fed 34 percent protein. Another study done on dogs with only one kidney showed that protein levels up to 44 percent of the diet had no harmful effect on the remaining kidney.[57]

You can find the full article, with references, at www.dogaware.com.

Pet food math

The basic math concept for analyzing any pet food is:

fat + protein + carbohydrate = 100% of calories

Most of us, including when we look at food labels on human food, tend to focus on the gross amount of fat, protein, and carbohydrates contained in the food we eat or feed our dogs. The best way to analyze any food is the way professional food scientists and formulators do—by looking at where the calories come from. In other words, they analyze foods on a caloric basis, and that's how I have analyzed the recipes in this book.

So given this perspective, it is not always easy to answer a question like "How much protein is in the dog food you feed?" The "guaranteed analyses" on bags of dog food do not tell you the most important information: the percentage of calories from protein and the grams of protein per 1,000 kcal. What I am going to show you in this section is how to take the guaranteed analysis information and calculate the protein, fat, and carbohydrate content on a "dry matter" (DM), percentage of calories and grams of nutrients on a per 1,000 kcal basis.

Guaranteed analyses: protein, fat, carbohydrate content.

All dog food and treat packages are required to include a guaranteed analysis, listing protein and fat as minimums, and fiber and moisture as maximums on an "as fed" basis. The guaranteed analyses are not complete, though, since they do not list the carbohydrate content of the food. This is important information—carbohydrate content is required on all human food labels—but pet food regulations do not allow the word "carbohydrate" on the label. So we need to calculate carbohydrates, and, fortunately, it's easy.

All dog foods consist of protein, fat, moisture, ash, and carbohydrate. The total of these components equals 100%. Ash is what's leftover if one cooks the food at very high temperatures; it is generally the mineral content of the food. Fiber is the part of the plant material that the dog cannot digest; it's considered to be a carbohydrate.

Carbohydrates, while not essential nutrients, are used in most dry dog foods as an inexpensive (relative to meat) source of calories.

Calculating carbohydrate content

Here is a typical guaranteed analysis for an adult dry food:

Minimum protein	26%
Minimum fat	15%
Maximum fiber	4%
Maximum moisture	10%

Keep in mind that the protein and fat figures are minimums only; few companies understate protein, but some may understate fat. Ash is usually not listed. Typical ash content of a dry food is in the 4 to 8% range, and we'll use 6% in our calculations. Even though fiber is a carbohydrate, we will subtract the fiber when calculating total digestible carbohydrate content because fiber provides no calories.

The FDA defines how to calculate carbohydrate: Subtract the weight of crude protein, total fat, moisture, and ash from the total weight ("wet weight") of the sample of food.[58]

Therefore, in our example, we calculate the carbohydrate content like this:

Carbohydrate contents= 100% – 26% – 15% – 10% – 6% = 43%.

In this example, carbohydrates include fiber. Subtract the fiber (4%) and the digestible carbohydrate content is 39%.

Comparing protein content of dry and canned or wet foods

To compare dry with wet foods, you must subtract the water content from the food content. Water, though absolutely essential, provides no calories, minerals, or vitamins. What remains after you remove the water is the dry matter (DM)—protein, fat, carbohydrate (including fiber), and ash. A DM analysis tells us the percentage of the DM that is protein, fat, and carbohydrate, and allows us to make more accurate comparisons between various types of foods.

The label of a typical canned dog food states:

Minimum protein	10%
Minimum fat	8%
Maximum fiber	3%
Maximum moisture	75%

Which has more protein, the dry food at 26% protein, or the canned food at 10% protein? Let's find out.

Step 1. Calculate the total dry matter in both foods by subtracting the percentage moisture from 100%.

Canned food, with 75% moisture, has 25% total dry matter (100% – 75%). If the can is 12 oz, 25% of the can, or 3 oz., is dry. The rest is moisture. Dry food, with 10% moisture, has 90% dry matter.

Step 2. Divide the listed protein percentage by the dry matter percentage.

Canned:

Listed protein: 10%. Divide 10% by 25% = 40% protein DM.

Dry:

Listed protein: 26%. Divide 26% by 90% = 29% protein DM.

The canned food has more protein than the dry food, even though the listed protein of the dry food is much higher. Protein is 40% of the dry matter of a typical canned food (listing 10%) and 29% of the dry matter of the dry food (listing 26%).

You can calculate the fat and carbohydrate content in the same manner. Table 8.3 compares the macronutrient content of the dry and canned foods above on dry matter basis. The carbohydrate content is the digestible portion only (total carbohydrate less fiber).

Table 8.3 Macronutrient content, dry matter basis

	Dry	**Canned**
Protein	27%	40%
Fat	16%	32%
Carbohydrate	41%	22%

Calculating percentage of calories

A better picture of the overall balance of the diet emerges when the actual percentage of calories from each nutrient is known. Human nutritionists almost always think in terms of the percentage of our calories that we get from fat. It is important information for pet foods as well.

Fat provides 8.5 to 9 kcal of metabolizable energy (the amount of usable energy obtained from the food by the dog) per gram, more than twice as much as carbohydrates and protein, which provide 3.5 to 4 kcal/gram, depending on the quality of the food. Human-quality foods are generally more digestible than pet quality foods, therefore they contain more energy. When calculating calories for human foods, food scientists use Atwater factors: 9 kcal/g of fat and 4 kcal/g of protein and carbohydrate. For animal foods, AAFCO requires that caloric content be calculated using modified Atwater factors: 8.5 kcal/g of fat, and 3.5 kcal/g of protein and carbohydrate because the ingredients are less digestible. In this book, I assumed all ingredients were human grade, and therefore all calculations used Atwater factors.

To determine the percentage of the calories from fat, protein, and carbohydrate multiply the "as fed" or listed percentage of protein and carbohydrate (less fiber) by 4; multiply the as fed fat content by

9; add the numbers together, and then take the percentage that each macronutrient provides. Here's an example, this time using a typical frozen raw food.

Analysis on the bag reads:

Minimum protein	13%
Minimum fat	10%
Maximum fiber	1%
Maximum moisture	74%

We'll estimate ash at 1.5% (about 6% on a dry matter basis), which is typical for raw beef and lamb diets; chicken based foods usually have a 2–3% ash content (Table 8.4).

Table 8.4 Commercial frozen raw diet, caloric contribution calculations

	As fed	Atwater factor	kcal in 1 gram of food	% of kcal
Protein	13%	4	0.52	36%
Fat	10%	9	0.9	63%
Ash	1.5%			
Moisture	74%			
Fiber	1%			
Digestible carbohydrates	0.5%	4	0.02	1%
Total	100%		1.44	100%

63% of the calories in this food are from fat, making this a very high-fat food, certainly when compared with dry foods and the ancestral diet. Even though this is a raw, meat-based food, with 36% of the calories from protein, it contains less protein than some of the high protein dry foods, as shown in Table 2.1 in Chapter 2.

Calculating amount of nutrients per 1,000 kcal.
As a food formulator, I analyze food on an amount of nutrient per 1,000 kcal basis. This is the AAFCO required method of analyzing high caloric content diets, which all meat-based diets are. A 45-pound dog will consume about 1,000 kcal per day.

It's easy to calculate amounts on a 1,000 kcal basis. In Table 8.4 above, we see that there are 1.44 kilocalories per gram of food, as fed. That means that there are 694 grams of food per 1,000 kcal (1000 kcal/1.44 kcal/g = 694 g).

To calculate the grams of protein and fat, multiply the "as fed" or listed percentage by 694 grams. 13% of 694 grams is 90, i.e., there are 90 grams of protein per 1,000 kcal. 10% of 694 is 69, i.e., there are 69 grams of fat per 1,000 kcal. If you have a typical 45-pound dog and fed this food, your dog would consume 90 grams of protein and 69 grams of fat. Table 8.5 compares the fat and protein content of various foods, including the recipes presented in Chapter 6.

Table 8.5 Grams of fat and protein per 1000 kcal, various foods

	Fat	Protein
Ancestral	49	123
Typical dry	35	63
High protein dry	48	95
Fatty commercial frozen	81	51
Typical commercial frozen	66	91
80% lean beef	80	69
93% lean beef	49	145
ABC beef recipe	50	124
ABC chicken recipe	48	121
The Perfect Fat Diet	49	124

Appendix A

FOUR HIGH PROTEIN, LOW-AND-BALANCED FAT RECIPES

Here are four high protein, low-and-balanced fat recipes for full time feeding I developed in conjunction with Mary Straus, published in the *Whole Dog Journal* (January, 2009). We developed these recipes for adult dogs needing low-fat diets, including dogs with pancreas issues. Approximately 43% of the calories come from protein, 22% from fat, and 35% from carbohydrate.

These high protein, low fat recipes may also be ideal for overweight and inactive dogs. Many recent studies have shown that high protein diets help dogs lose weight (see Chapter 1 for details). These recipes are not for puppies, pregnant bitches, or lactating bitches because they are too low in fat and minerals to meet their needs.

Recipe #1: Chicken (no bones)
    14 oz chicken thighs, skin and separable fat removed
    1 lb sweet potato, baked in skin
    ½ lb broccoli stalks
    2 oz chicken liver
    1 oz chicken heart (or use 3 oz of liver and no heart)
    1 level tsp eggshell powder
    ¼ tsp iodized salt
    40 to 120 IUs (2 to 6 drops) vitamin E

This recipe yields 1,007 kcal (24 kcal/oz) and has 22 grams of fat per 1,000 kcal. The overall (including short and long chain) omega-6:-3 ratio is 7:1.

Recipe #2: Beef

12 oz ground beef, 95% lean
12 oz white rice, cooked
6 oz red leaf lettuce
1 oz beef liver
1 oz beef heart
1½ tsp bonemeal
¾ tsp hempseed oil (can substitute ¾ tsp walnut oil or 1½ tsp canola oil)
¼ tsp cod liver oil
¼ tsp kelp
20 to 100 IUs (1 to 5 drops) vitamin E

This recipe yields 1,015 kcal (24 kcal/oz) and has 24 grams of fat per 1,000 kcal. The omega-6:-3 ratio is 4:1.

Recipe #3: Mixed, chicken (no bones) and beef

3 lbs whole wheat macaroni, cooked
2 lbs chicken thighs, skin and separable fat removed
1 lb ground beef, 95% lean
1 lb broccoli stalks
1 lb red leaf lettuce
½ lb chicken liver
½ lb beef heart
1 can (3½ oz) sardines
Egg white from 1 large egg
4 tsp eggshell powder (or 6,000 mg calcium from other sources)
1 tsp kelp meal
200+ IUs (10+ drops) vitamin E

This recipe yields 4,206 kcal (28 kcal/oz) and has 24 grams of fat per 1,000 kcal. The omega-6:-3 ratio is 5:1.

Recipe #4: Chicken with bones (serve raw)

6 oz chicken necks, skin and separable fat removed
½ lb chicken thighs, skin and separable fat removed
1 lb sweet potato, baked in skin
½ lb broccoli stalks
3 oz chicken liver
¼ tsp iodized salt
40 to 100 IUs (2 to 5 drops) vitamin E

This recipe yields 995 kcal (24 kcal/oz) and has 24 grams of fat per 1,000 kcal. The omega-6:-3 ratio is 7:1. This recipe must be served raw.

Feeding Amounts: The amount to feed based on the four recipes will vary considerably depending upon your dog's activity level and metabolism. The chart below shows how much to feed older, inactive dogs.

Dog's weight, pounds	Daily kcal require-ments, older dogs	Ounces per day to feed
5	150	6
15	340	14
25	500	21
45	770	32
75	1100	47
100	1400	58

Substitutions: Almost any green vegetables can be substituted for those listed. However, chicken breast meat cannot be substituted for the thigh meat without upsetting the fat balance. Chicken thigh meats are higher in the long chain omega-3s than breast meat. Any form of calcium can be substituted for eggshell powder at the rate of 1,500 mg calcium per level tsp of eggshell powder. You can also substitute bonemeal for eggshell, but you need to use more bonemeal than eggshell because of the phosphorus in bonemeal. Substitute 1½ to 2 tsp bonemeal (6 to 8 grams) per 1 tsp of eggshell powder, and vice versa.

Appendix B

SOURCES OF DATA AND THE ANALYSIS PROGRAM

I analyzed the recipes in this book using a nutrient analysis program that I developed and extensively tested with commercial laboratory chemical testing. The program includes over 750 ingredients, and analyzes recipes for macronutrients, vitamins, minerals, fatty acids, and amino acids. Most of the data come from the *USDA National Nutrient Database for Standard Reference,* Releases 18–20. For the foods not listed in the USDA database (primarily chicken wings, necks, backs and turkey necks) I used results of the macronutrient and mineral tests I conducted for Steve's Real Food and other pet food companies, supplier data, and published data from the BARF-world website.[59]

The USDA database does not provide sufficient data for chloride (Cl), iodine (I), and vitamins D and E. In all of the chemical tests on foods I formulated, lack of Cl was never a problem; nonetheless I include ample sources of Cl in some of the recipes. Likewise, I include sources of iodine and vitamins D and E. The USDA data on choline content are not complete; the values presented should be considered minimums.

The nutrient analyses are general guidelines only. The vitamin and mineral content of natural foods varies up to 30% based on variety, soil conditions, growth enhancers used, post-harvest treatments, and other factors. Nutrient bioavailability (how well the nutrient is used by the body) is not considered, just gross intake. Bioavailability varies according to many factors, including the food consumed with the nutrient. Some plant foods contain anti-nutritional factors, including oxalates, phytates, and tannates, that inhibit the absorption of some of the minerals.

How accurate is chemical testing?

I've had more than 100 ingredients or full recipes tested at five different testing laboratories in the USA. I have found mistakes, some significant, from every lab. I've concluded that laboratory chemical testing is not sufficient in analyzing diets, unless confirmed by computer analyses. Here are just two examples of why I write this.

In 2007, I sent mechanically skinned chicken necks to a nutrient-testing laboratory in California. When I got the results of the first test, I called the lab and told them that the results did not make sense, especially the 0.02% calcium (Ca) in chicken necks without skin. I asked for a retest. I sent them more skinned chicken necks, from the same batch. The second results came back meeting my calcium and fat expectations (column 2, Table B.1), but the phosphorus still did not make sense. Bone contains 2 to 3 parts Ca to 1 part phosphorus (P); the Ca:P ratio on chicken necks with meat should be less than 2:1. So I asked for a third test and, finally, this test came back with credible results.

Table B.1 Test results for mechanically skinned chicken necks

	Test one, 3/22/07	Test two, 4/17/07	Test three, 4/27/07
Protein	14.80%	16.94%	17.32%
Fat	14.24%	5.78%	5.21%
Moisture	70.74%	71.18%	72.09%
Ca	0.02%	1.9%	1.7%
P	0.1%	0.23%	1.23%

The next time I wanted to test products I went to a different laboratory, this one in the middle of the US. A client wanted me to fine-tune his formulas. His company has five varieties of food. All have the same meat to vegetable percentages, and used the same vegetables. Therefore, I expected the protein and fat content of the various diets to differ, based upon the leanness of the meats, but the carbohydrate and fiber content should be identical with all five diets. All the carbohydrate and fiber comes from the plants. Table B.2 shows the first results from the chemical testing by one of the most respected labs in the country. The laboratory results showed that food D has more than three times the carbohydrate content of food A and E. That is not possible.

Table B.2 Reported percentages of protein, fat, fiber, and carbohydrate

	Food A	Food B	Food C	Food D	Food E
Protein	57	54	49	29	57
Fat	28	21	19	31	18
Fiber	1.5	1.4	1.4	1.4	1.5
Carbohydrate	9	20	14	31	8

Needless to say, nutrient testing is an inexact science. We must make the best reasoned decisions we can with the data available, which is what I've tried to do in this book.

Appendix C

ABBREVIATIONS

AA	arachidonic acid
AAFCO	Association of American Feed Control Officials
ALA	alpha-linolenic acid
Ca	calcium
Cl	chloride
CLA	conjugated linoleic acid
CQ-10	coenzyme Q-10
Cu	copper
DHA	docosahexaenoic acid
DM	dry matter
DPA	docosapentaenoic acid
EFAs	essential fatty acids
EPA	eicosapentaenoic acid
FDA	Food and Drug Administration
Fe	iron

g	gram
GLA	gamma linolenic acid
I	iodine
IUs	International Units
K	potassium
kcal	kilocalorie, often referred to as Calorie (1,000 calories)
kg	kilogram
LA	linoleic acid
lb	pound
LC n-3	long chain (more than 18 carbon atoms) omega-3 fatty acids
LC n-6	long chain (more than 18 carbon atoms) omega-6 fatty acids
mg	milligram, 1/1,000 of a gram
Mg	magnesium
Mn	manganese
MUFAs	monounsaturated fatty acids
n-3	omega-3 fatty acid
n-6	omega-6 fatty acid
Na	sodium
NRC	National Research Council of the National Academies
P	phosphorus
PS	phosphatidylserine
PUFAs	polyunsaturated fatty acids
oz	ounce
Se	selenium

SFAs   saturated fatty acids

tsp   teaspoon

USDA   United States Department of Agriculture

Zn   zinc

18-c   18-carbon fatty acid

RECOMMENDED READING

Fats

Fats are at the leading edge of nutrition, so it's important to read the latest information from knowledgeable authors. Readers wanting more information about fats, and about the effect of fats on the brain, will find these books interesting.

Susan Allport, *The Queen of Fats: why Omega-3s were removed from the western diet and what we can do to replace them.* U California Press, 2006.

Michael Schmidt, *Brain-Building Nutrition: The Healing Power of Fats and Oils.* Frog Ltd., 2001.

Mary Enig, *Know Your Fats: The Complete Primer for Understanding the Nutrition of Fats, Oils and Cholesterol.* Bethesda Press, 2002.

Raw Feeding

For those wanting to learn more about feeding raw meat based diets to their dogs, I recommend, of course, my first book; Dr. Richard Pitcairn's latest book; and the NRC 2006 report (very expensive, it's best to order this book through a library). Dogwise Publishing offers a wide variety of books on raw feeding, www.dogwise.com.

Steve Brown and Beth Taylor, *See Spot Live Longer: How to help your dog live a longer and healthier life!* Creekobear Press, 2004.

Dr. Richard Pitcairn, *Complete Guide to Natural Health for Dogs and Cats, Third Edition.* Rodale Books, 2005.

Subcommittee on Dog and Cat Nutrition, Committee on Animal Nutrition, National Research Council of the National Academies (NRC), *Nutrient Requirements of Dogs and Cats,* 2006.

Authors who have studied fats for many years include Barry Sears, author of *The Zone Diet* and Artemis Simopoulos, author of *The Omega Plan.* Their information about fats is relevant for dogs and humans.

Three websites with newsletters that have good information on fats are www.vitalchoice.com, www.thepaleodiet.com, and www.mercola.com.

CITATIONS

[1]Landry SM, Van Ruining HJ. "The diet of feral carnivores: a review of stomach content analysis." *J Am Animal Hosp Assoc.* 1979 Nov/Dec; 15:775-781.

[2]Coppinger R, Coppinger L. *Dogs: A Startling New Understanding of Canine Origin, Behavior & Evolution.* 2001.

[3]Puotinen CJ. "What a wolf eats: research on wild canids can help inform dietary planning for dogs." *Whole Dog Journal.* 2005; 8(3).

[4]Stahler D, Smith D, Guernsey D. "Foraging and Feeding Ecology of the Gray Wolf (Canis lupus): Lessons from Yellowstone National Park, Wyoming, USA." *J. Nutr.* 2006 July; 136:1923S-1926S.

[5]Darimont C. et al. "Spawning salmon disrupt trophic coupling between wolves and ungulate prey in coastal British Columbia." *BMC Ecology.* 2008; 8:14.

[6]Dierenfeld ES, Alcorn HL, Jacobsen KL. "Nutrient composition of whole vertebrate prey (excluding fish) fed in zoos." *Zoo Biology.* 1996;15:525 -537.

[7]Dierenfeld, 1996.

[8]Brown S. A. "Macronutrient and Mineral Comparison of Three Popular Homemade Raw Food Diet Plans with NRC and Ancestral Diet Nutrient Profiles; and Suggestions on How to Enhance Nutritional Compliance with Both." *JAHVMA*. 2007 Jan; 22 (4) 9-16..

[9]Brown S. A. 2007.

[10]Hand, Thatcher, Remillard, Roudebush. *Small Animal Clinical Nutrition IV,* Mark Morris Associates. 2000; 66.

[11]*NRC.* 2006. 207.

[12]Addis PB. "Occurrence of lipid oxidation products in foods." *Food Chem Toxicol.* 1986 Oct-Nov; 2410-11): 1021-30.

[13]Pokorný J, Janícek G. "Interaction between proteins and oxidized lipids." *Nahrung.* 1975; 19(9-10): 911-20.

[14]Enig M. *Know Your Fats: The Complete Primer for Understanding the Nutrition of Fats, Oils and Cholesterol.* 2000; 230.

[15]Houssier M, Raoul W, Lavalette S, Keller N, Guillonneau X, et al. "CD36 deficiency leads to choroidal involution via COX2 downregulation in rodents." *PLoS Med.* 2008; 5(2): e39.

[16]Banwart G. *Basic Food Microbiology, 2nd ed.* 1989: 7.

[17]Hermann Esterbauer. "Cytotoxicity and genotoxicity of lipid-oxidation products." Am J Clin Nutr. 1193;57: 779S-86S.

[18]Halliwell, B. Gutteridge, J. *Free Radicals in Biology and Medicine, 2nd ed.* 1989: 208.

[19]Robert C. Backus, Kwang Suk Ko, Andrea J. Fascetti, Mark D. Kittleson, Kristin A. MacDonald, David J. Maggs, John R. Berg, and Quinton R. Rogers. "Low Plasma Taurine Concentration in Newfoundland Dogs is Associated with Low Plasma Methionine and Cyst(e)ine Concentrations and Low Taurine Synthesis." *J. Nutr.,* Oct 2006; 136: 2525-2533.

[20]Weaver et al. "Effect of dietary fatty acids on inflammatory gene expression in healthy humans." *Journal of Biological Chemistry,* 2009. Retrieved June 2, 2009, from http://www.sciencedaily.com/releases/2009/05/090529183250.htm

[21]University of California—Los Angeles Scientists Learn How Food Affects The Brain: Omega 3 Especially Important." (2008, July 11). *Science Daily.* Retrieved July 14, 2008 from http://www.sciencedaily.com /releases/2008/07/080709161922.htm.

[22]For complete references, I refer the reader to three recently published review articles that reference the hundreds of studies upon which these conclusions were built. Gomez-Pinilla, Fernando "Brain Foods: the effects of nutrients on brain fuction." *Nature Reviews Neuroscience.* 9, 568–578 (July 2008); McCann, Joyce and Ames, Bruce "Is docosahexaenoic acid...required for development of normal brain function? An overview of evidence from cognitive and behavioral tests in humans and animals." *Am J Clin Nutr.* 2005;82: 281–95; and Carlson, Susan "Early determinants of development: a lipid perspective." *Am J Clin Nutr.* 2009;89(suppl):1523S–9S.

[23]Carl Julien, Cyntia Tremblay, Alix Phivilay, Line Berthiaume, Pierre Julien, Frédéric Calon. "High-fat diet aggravates amyloid-beta and tau pathologies in the 3xTg-AD mouse model." *Neurobiology of Aging.* October 2008.

[24]Hill-Baskin, A.E. et al. "Diet-induced hepatocellular carcinoma in genetically-predisposed mice." *Human Molecular Genetics* Advance Access published online on May 19, 2009.

[25]Milgram N.W. et al. "Learning ability in aged beagle dogs is preserved by behavioral enrichment and dietary fortification: a two-year longitudinal study." *Neurobiology of Aging.* 26; 2005 77-90.

[26]Hannah SS, Laflamme DP. "Increased dietary protein spared lean body mass during weight loss in dogs." Presented at the ACVIM 16th Annual VeterinaryMedical Forum, 1998.

[27]Nodtvedt A et al. "A case-control study of risk factors for canine atopic dermatitis among boxer, bullterrier and West Highland white terrier dogs in Sweden." *Veterinary Dermatology.* 2007 Oct;18(5) 309-315.

[28]Baily G. "When you look at the experimental animal data, it's very clear that many components of fruits and, especially, vegetables are protective in a large number of models. The isothiocyanates in cruciferous vegetables…are effective in many animals models." *Linus Pauling Institute Research Newsletter.* 2008 spring; 6.

[29]Hickman MA, Roger QR, Morris JG. "Effect of processing on the fate of dietary taurine in cats." *J Nutr.* 1990; 120: 995-1000.

[30]Brown S, Taylor B. *See Spot Live Longer, How to help your dog live a longer and healthier life!* 2004; 58.

[31]Vaisman et al. "Correlation between changes in blood fatty acid composition and visual sustained attention performance in children with inattention: effect of dietary n-3 fatty acids containing phospholipids." *Am J Clin Nutr.* 2008; 87:1170–80; and Visoli F, Risé P, et al. Dietary Intake of Fish vs. Formulations Leads to Higher Plasma Concentrations of n-3 Fatty Acids. *Lipids* 2003; 38 (4): 415-423.

[32]Song JH, Inoue Y, Miyazawa, T. "Oxidative stability of docosahexaenoic acid-containing oils in the form of phospholipids, triacylglycerols, and ethyl esters." *Biosci Biotechnol Biochem.* 1997 Dec; 61(12):2085-8.

[33]From private conversations with Dr. Ken Hildebrand, marine biologist at Oregon State University, Corvallis, OR and Dr. James Morris, University of California at Davis. September 2000.

[34]*Mother Earth News.* October/November 2007.

[35]Song, 1997.

[36]Ahlstrøm O, Krogdahl Å, Vhile S. "Fatty Acid Composition in Commercial Dog Foods." *J. Nutr.* 2004 Aug; 134:2145S-2147S.

[37]Billinghurst, I. "Calcium and Energy Sources for Growing Dogs." *Carnivora,* 2002; 1(2) 13.

[38]Calculated assuming 6.5% bone in a typical prey animal, with hydroxyapatite being 70% of the bone. The mineral phase of bone is composed mostly of calcium hydroxyapatite ($Ca_{10}(PO_4)6(OH_2)$, which has a Ca:P ratio of 2.15:1 by weight (1.67:1 on a molar basis).

[39]*NRC.* 208.

[40]University of Montreal. "Pregnant Women Consuming Flaxseed Oil Have High Risk Of Premature Birth." 2008, October 29, *ScienceDaily.* Retrieved November 4, 2008, from http://www.sciencedaily.com /releases/2008/10/081027140817.htm.

[41]Esterbauer, Hermann. "Cytotoxicity and genotoxicity of lipid-oxidation problems." *Am J Clin Nutr.* 1993;57(suppl): 779S-86S.

[42]Bingham, Phillips, and Bauer. "Potential for dietary protection against the effects of aflatoxins in animals." *Journal of the American Veterinary Medical Association,* Vol. 222, No. 5. March 1, 2003. 593.

[43]The data we've seen from manufacturers of antimicrobials shows that after four days at above 12% moisture mold growth starts.

[44]Hughes, Graham & Grieb "Overt Signs of Toxicity to Dogs and Cats of Dietary Deoxynivalenol." *Journal of Animal Sciences,* 1999. 77: 699-700.

[45]Chafee and Himes, "Aflatoxicosis in Dogs." *American Journal of Veterinary Research,* Vol 30, No 10, October 1969. 1748.

[46]Council for Agricultural Science and Technology, Ames, Iowa, USA. *Mycotoxins: Risks in Plant, Animal, and Human Systems.* January 2003. 32.

[47]http://www.fsis.usda.gov/Fact_Sheets/Focus_On_Freezing/index.asp#12.

[48]Bauer, J, Dunbar, B, Bigley, K. "Dietary Flaxseed in Dogs Results in Differential Transport and Metabolism of (n-3) Polyunsaturated Fatty Acids." *J. Nutr,* 1998; 128: 2641S-2644S.

[49]*NRC,* 88-89.

[50]Banwart G. *Basic food Microbiology, 2nd ed.* 1989; 7.

[51]Case L, Carey D, Hirakawa D. *Canine and Feliine Nutrition,* Mosby 1995; 93.

[52]Hand, Thatcher, Remillard, Roudebush. *Small Animal Clinical Nutrition IV,* Mark Morris Associates 2000; 41.

[53]Burger I, ed. *The Waltham Book of Companion Animal Nutrition,* Pergamon 1995; 10.

[54]*NRC,* 2006; 59.

[55]Association of American Feed Control Officials, *Official Publication,* 2003. 178.

[56]Markwell, P.J., *Applied Clinical Nutrition of the Dog and Cat. A Guide to Waltham® Veterinary Diets.* 1998. 38.

[57]Straus, M. "New research is changing the way the senior dog's diet is maintained." *Whole Dog Journal.* 2006 December.

[58]http://www.cfsan.fda.gov/~dms/flg-5-2.html 21. *CFR* 101.9(c)(6).

[59]BARFWORLD, http://www.barfworld.com/html/barfworld/analysis.html. Accessed on 5 December 2006.

INDEX

ABOUT THE AUTHOR

Steve Brown started working with dogs in the early 1980s trying to develop Charlee Bear® Dogs: 40 pound, non-shedding dogs bred "to give and receive love." Working with leading canine geneticists and behaviorists, he developed a long term breeding plan for the dogs. In 1992, understanding that positive reinforcement training techniques were required to enhance teddy bear traits, he developed a best-selling low-calorie training treat (Charlee Bear® Dog Treats), still one of the best selling dog treats in the nation. In the early 1990s Brown realized that he was not finding the hybrid vigor in some of his dogs that he expected, and he started focusing on diet. In 1998, he developed Steve's Real Food® for Pets, the first AAFCO-compliant, frozen, raw meat-based diet. After developing national distribution, Brown left the company to focus on research and education. In 2004, Brown co-authored a book on canine nutrition, *See Spot Live Longer,* now in its seventh printing, and has published more than 30 articles on canine nutrition on leading natural health web sites and in pet related magazines and veterinary journals.

Steve Brown lives in Eugene, Oregon with his Charlee Bear dogs. Steve can be contacted through his website www.seespotlivelonger. com.

Also available from Dogwise Publishing

Go to www.dogwise.com for more books and ebooks.

Raw Dog Food
Make it Easy for You and Your Dog!
Carina Beth MacDonald

In an era of poisonous pet food with ingredients that can kill, home-prepared diets make even more sense. Learn why and how to feed your dog a diet that mimics what wild canids eat—raw meat and bones.

Raw Meaty Bones
Tom Lonsdale

Feeding a natural, unprocessed diet is needed now more than ever. A complete and authoritative reference on the benefits of a raw food diet for your dog. Written by an Australian vet and leader in raw feeding, this well researched book provides a suggested diet, feeding tips, and do's and don'ts.

Work Wonders
Feed Your Dog Raw Meaty Bones
Tom Lonsdale

Get rid of doggy breath! Written by a leader in the raw pet food movement, you'll learn the essentials of feeding your dog including how to find sources, store, and prepare a healthy diet.

Performance Dog Nutrition
Optimize Performance with Nutrition
Dr. Jocelynn Jacobs

Get better performance from your canine athlete! Learn how to meet the special nutritional needs of your performance dog and how to meet them with a sound nutrition program. Explains how to read dog food labels and select appropriate food for your dog.

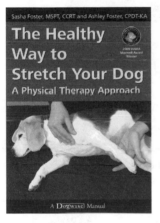

The Healthy Way to Stretch Your Dog
A Physical Therapy Approach
Sasha Foster, MSPT, CCRT and Ashley Foster, CPDT-KA

You have probably heard that humans need to stretch for good health. So do dogs. Now you can learn how to safely and effectively stretch your dog to prevent injuries, maintain joint integrity, and improve your dog's fitness, whether he is an elite canine athlete or a lap dog.

Canine Massage, 2nd Ed.
A Complete Reference Manual
Jean-Pierre Hourdebaigt, L.M.T.

Bring the well-known benefits of massage to your own dog or become a canine massage specialist. Over 100 illustrations and 100 photos, detailed examinations of muscular stress points, diagnoses, and treatments.

Dogwise.com your source for quality books, ebooks, DVDs, training tools and treats.

We've been selling to the dog fancier for more than 25 years and we carefully screen our products for quality information, safety, durability and FUN! You'll find something for every level of dog enthusiast on our website www.dogwise.com or drop by our store in Wenatchee, Washington.